ANDREAS VESALIUS

THE MAKING, THE MADMAN, AND THE MYTH

STEPHEN N. JOFFE

authorHOUSE®

AuthorHouse™ LLC
1663 Liberty Drive
Bloomington, IN 47403
www.authorhouse.com
Phone: 1-800-839-8640

Published by AuthorHouse 03/20/2014

ISBN: 978-1-4918-7447-9 (sc)
ISBN: 978-1-4918-7445-5 (hc)
ISBN: 978-1-4918-7446-2 (e)

Library of Congress Control Number: 2014905222

TABLE OF CONTENTS

SECTION THREE: THE MYTH

Genius lives on, all else is mortal.[1]

—Andreas Vesalius

INTRODUCTION

THERE IS A CLASSIC TALE told of a man who, after many years of isolation, comes down from a mountain to liberate the townspeople of their misconceived lives.[2] As the one who knows the Truth, the man runs amongst the people, explaining that they can be *free* if they will only look to see the lies that are oppressing them. Unable to hear the man's enlightened words, the townspeople mock him, throw stones at his head, and call him a madman. Unable to move his audience, the man, disillusioned and frustrated, returns to his home in the mountains, asking, *"Must one first smash their ears so that they learn to hear with their eyes?"*[3] Such is the story of the famed sixteenth-century anatomist, Andreas Vesalius.

Europe of the early Renaissance is romantically thought of as a time of light and rebirth, when humanist and religious reformation promised to liberate the populace from the dark repression of the past. But for those living through these formative years, the prospect of change brought with it both exhilaration and profound fear—the world was changing, and so were their places within it. There is thus a temptation, when speaking of the great expressions of "genius" engendered within the Renaissance, to reduce the lives of the innovators and artisans to the products that they created. It is my position, however, that if we allow our attention to be primarily absorbed by material achievements, then we will overlook what is most critical about their work. Although Andreas Vesalius is remembered mainly for his incredible accomplishment of creating an illustrated medical text unlike anything ever seen before, his genius, his vision, and his courage are the real story.

In the practice of medicine, the Renaissance saw the classic medical scholars of antiquity deified and staunchly deemed infallible and irreproachable. Like the enchanting songs of the sirens, their authoritative voices were so deafening that even one's eyes could be fooled into believing that they could see what was not truly there. For the "madmen," however, who like Vesalius were able to silence the noise of the past, a new reality appeared. Through the insistent performance of dissection, Vesalius created a silent refuge for himself in the raw physical anatomy of the human body—an act that quite literally gave him sight. The following account is not so much a biography as it is a story of the madman who did not return to the mountain but who instead, through the development of an astounding book, created a silence in the field of medicine that would allow others, too, to see.

Andreas Vesalius, a pioneer of medical study and the most influential anatomist of the sixteenth century, advocated disciplined and detailed studies of the human body that became a mantra for his method of anatomical discovery: the only way to learn the true nature of the body is to cut into it with one's own hands and to observe with one's own eyes the truths revealed through dissection.

In 1543, Vesalius published his magnum opus, *De humani corporis fabrica (The Structure of the Human Body)*—a manuscript that can well be credited for the momentum of the modern medical principles of research, discovery, and empiricism. By exploring the intriguing life of Andreas Vesalius and his *Fabrica*, one finds not only the details of a fascinating personal history but a vivid expression of the social forces and vital elements that gave birth to the modern world.

It is not the intention of this book to present the reader with a full biography of the sixteenth-century anatomist—Vesalius scholar, C. D. O'Malley, has already succeeded at that task—but to take the reader on a journey through the life and experiences of a great and entirely unique character in medical history.

The manuscript is divided into three parts: Section one, "The Making," contextualizes the life and work of Andreas Vesalius by orienting his familial inheritance and his conventional education amidst the innovations and influential intellectual movements of his time; section two, "The Madman," demonstrates how Vesalius, forced by war to change his course of study, cast off the husks of tradition and expectation and materialized as a profoundly revolutionary anatomist. In a move that would align the study of medicine to the study of the body, Vesalius's illustrated anatomical manuscript, the *Fabrica*, showed the human body as it had never before been imagined. In the aftermath of its hugely successful publication, Vesalius was categorically deemed a "madman" (*Vaesani*) by some and a genius by others. In the third and final section of this history, "The Myth," Vesalius appears as a tragic hero who, through the conditions engendered by a grievous "error," comes to recognize his own true potential. But in the ill humor of the fates, just as Vesalius is about to take his true place in the history of medicine, his circumstances turn fatally tragic.

There are moments in the history of humanity when an event occurs that is so extraordinary and unexpected that the world, for better or for worse, is changed forever. The appearance of Vesalius's *De humani corporis fabrica* in 1543 marks one of these times. Through the creation of a series of images drawn from firsthand observations of that which is most intimate to the individual, his anatomy, Vesalius presented to his audience the paradox of life and death in all of its glory and absurdity. By creating a space—a book—where words break down and the authority of the patriarchs is muted, Vesalius inscribed himself into the future of medicine and the world by forcing his audience to listen not with their ears—but with their eyes.

SECTION ONE: THE MAKING

They must find it difficult, those who have taken authority as the truth, rather than truth as the authority.
—Gerald Massey

It can be argued that Andreas Vesalius and his significance to medicine and scientific study were as much the product of his family heritage and historical timing as they were the result of his individual drive, insight, and genius. Section one introduces the reader to the making of Vesalius by situating his youth and early education within the context of strong determining external influences.

CHAPTER ONE

A Man of His Family

Brussels, 1514

IN THE EARLY MORNING OF December 31, in the final hours of another "year of our Lord," Andries and Isabel van Wesele welcomed the birth of their second son, Andreas van Wesele.[4] Although medically trained, the child's father was decidedly absent from the important event of the birth despite being fairly close at hand. Andreas Vesalius entered the world within the warmth of the family home, a house that had been given to his father, Andries, on the occasion of his marriage to Vesalius's mother, Isabel Crabbe. The homestead was located within the *quartier de la Haute-Rue*, the quarter of the High Street, one of the two oldest thoroughfares in Brussels along Helle Straetken, Hell's Lane, in the neighborhood of the Sablon church. Consequently, the young Wesele family resided in a modest but respectable neighborhood close to the Coudenberg Palace. Over the preceding hundred years, the population of this district had increased steadily, attracting well-to-do merchants, aristocrats, and Vesalius's father, the personal apothecary to the court of Margaret of Austria. Indeed, holding this imperial position had been the hindrance preventing Andries from attending his son's birth, for within a few days, on January 6, at the Feast of the Epiphany, Emperor Maximilian planned to ceremoniously declare his grandson, Charles V, Duke of Burgundy and King of Castile, to be of age to receive his birthright and formally assume governance over the

Burgundian Low Countries. It is reasonable that as personal apothecary to the court of Margaret of Austria, Andries was required at the Coudenberg Palace during this occasion.

The Wesele house was located between the two walls that encircled the city. The inner wall had been built in the twelfth century, but due to extensive population growth, the city's perimeter had been expanded, forcing a second outer wall to be built in the fourteenth century. As a young boy, Vesalius had opportunity to play in the large open fields close to his home and in the wooded hills that presented a vista of the entire city below. Vesalius would later reminisce that the woods provided him a bounty of vermin and woodland creatures with which he could develop his skills of dissection. Of particular interest is the fact that the Wesele family home was located close to Galgenberg, the Palaise de Justice, nicknamed Gallows Hill. Being so near the site of the city's public hangings, Vesalius was, from a young age, not only witness to numerous executions but was also given the opportunity to study, with the curiosity of youth, the bodies of the criminals that had been left to hang and rot. Leaving the bodies to decompose in the open was meant to warn the deviant citizenry not to offend the laws of justice; however, to a boy born into a family of physicians, the frequent sight of human bones and decaying flesh was a fascinating opportunity for examination.

In addition to these attractive qualities of Vesalius's hometown, Brussels also offered its citizens a unique and dynamic economy and animated cultural backdrop. Located on the River Senne, sixteenth-century Brussels was a center of government and industry, owing much of its commercial growth and economic prosperity to several centuries of textiles and tapestry manufacturing. The city was a nucleus of enterprise and culture, attracting merchants, craftsman, and some of the most accomplished artisans of northern Europe. Although Brussels had not yet demonstrated the volume or variety of commercial success characteristic of some other port cities, such as Bruges and Antwerp, its strategic location between the trade routes of Bruges and Cologne made it an essential inland trade route between northern Europe and the Mediterranean.

The pride and dignity of Brussels was as manifest in its architecture as it was in the consciousness of its citizenry. Having gained its political independence from the monarch, the city began construction of a glorious town hall in 1402 to commemorate the event. By 1444, the city's size had doubled, and gilded houses and large urban estates were constructed around the city's central square, La Grand-Place, where the opulent and ceremonious Cathedral of Saint Gudule would be erected in 1516. The seemingly omnipotent presence of the church's three-hundred-foot bell tower was amplified by the sixteen-foot copper statue of Saint Michael that stood upon it, his gaze looking mindfully over the small, impish *mannekeen pis*[5] fountain circulating water for the amusement of passersby. Daily, the magnificent bells and clocks that rang through out the bustling city ordered the activities of the citizens, merchants, artisans, housemaids, and travelers.

In addition to its robust economy, Vesalius's Brussels was also known throughout Europe for its progressive educational institutions and its intellectual community, making it competitive with the academic strongholds of northern Italy's Padua and Bologna.

While the independence, intellectual fertility, and creative openness of Brussels played a significant role in Vesalius's life, his noble family pedigree put his feet firmly on the path toward a career in the medical arts. Each of Vesalius's four forefathers had a distinguished career in medicine, and each was recognized for his expertise by being summoned to take up service within the Royal Courts of his day. It is thus without dispute that Vesalius's birthright was to establish himself not only as a prestigious physician but as one whose brilliance would culminate in an invitation to imperial service.

The Wesele family tradition began with Vesalius's great-great-grandfather, Peter van Wesele, who was known for having written a learned thesis on the fourth *fen* (section) of Avicenna's *Canon* (980-1036 CE), an encyclopedic text of Greek and Arabic medicine that remained in wide circulation until the seventeenth century. Vesalius would later develop an acute interest in his great-great-grandfather's work on the forth *fen* concerning the unpopular medical treatment known as *surgery*. Unfortunately, little is known about Vesalius's great-great-grandfather independent of Vesalius's own words on the man, which appear in a 1546 publication, *Letter on the China Root*. In it, Vesalius suggests that Peter van

Wesele attended to Emperor Fredrick III; however, because this fact cannot be formally verified, some scholars feel that it represents family legend rather than a legitimate truth.[6] Nonetheless, Vesalius appears to have believed it to be true; thus, a discussion of his "making" and his family's legacy of royal service must begin with Peter van Wesele.

Vesalius's great-grandfather, Johannes de Wesalia—unlike Johannes's father, Peter—left behind documented accounts of his distinguished academic career. Johannes first appears formally as a physician in the matriculation lists of the University of Louvain. Chartered in 1425 by the Duke of Brabant—Papal Bull in hand—Louvain had already become a recognized institution when Johannes arrived in 1429. Although Louvain was not the most established university in northern Europe, it did enjoy the benefits of ample municipal backing and private funding, which enabled it to attract many leading scholars of the day and secure an elevated reputation.

The archives from Louvain's university registry record Johannes's signature as *"Johannes de Wesali, doctor in medicines."* The title, "doctor of medicine," suggests that prior to arriving at Louvain, Johannes had already received a degree or medical *licentiate* from some university, but it is not known which one. That he was expected to assume substantial teaching responsibilities upon his arrival at Louvain suggests that Johannes graduated from a prestigious medical school, most likely the University of Paris. Johannes would come to play a significant role in both the history of Louvain and in the creation of Vesalius's own identity, for Master Johannes was not only a gifted scholar but a transformative thinker who would, in his time, change the direction of Louvain's curriculum for generations.

The faculty at Louvain invited Johannes to instruct a course in mathematics, as he had previously demonstrated a significant aptitude for the subject, in addition to more conventional studies in medicine. Although this may appear to be a fairly benign request, it is important to understand that traditionally a course in mathematics during the Renaissance focused primarily on applications of astrology, even within the field of medicine. The structuring belief system of academic ideology was based on the assumption that access to God—and, therefore, truth—came from understanding the laws of nature that he had put into place and that nowhere was this microcosm of divine purpose so pronounced as in the order and movements of the heavens. Thus, an individual's thorough understanding of astrology allowed for profound insight into the operation and function of all terrestrial life—from crop performance to civic and state affairs. It was thus common practice for astrological knowledge to be applied to the prevention and prognosis of illness and disease. The fundamental assumption of medical astrology was that illness and disease were symptomatic of a discontinuity between the order of the body and the order of nature, a state that could be determined by astrological computations. Therefore, the astrology of medicine—the "mathematics" that Johannes was asked to teach—entailed instructing students on how to calculate and predict the course of a disease by relating particular functions of the body to specific celestial configurations.[7] Signaling what would become a profound turn in the ideological direction of Louvain's school of medicine, Johannes declined the offer, preferring to focus his attention on the instruction of medical fact, rather than superstition.

Over the course of his career at Louvain, Johannes rose to the equivalent position of dean of the medical school. Aligning the curriculum and teaching methods with his own scientific values, he quickly transformed Louvain's medical program into one recognized as a progressive and decidedly grounded institute for learning. Although nearly a century would lapse before Vesalius himself would enter Louvain's school of medicine, it is likely that in most respects the curriculum remained much as Johannes had left it. Academic change at Louvain was not, it seemed, a reflection of developments in the field of medicine at large; rather, it was the product of radical innovators who would arrive in staggered succession across broad time spans.

In addition to his academic service, Johannes served as Brussels's city physician for many years and oversaw the dispensation of public health services and provisions for the poor. Johannes eventually left his civic position and entered the service of Emperor Frederick III of the House of Burgundy, just as his father (supposedly) had before him. It was during this period of imperial service that the emperor awarded the Wesele[8] family the heraldic insignia of the three weasels, a symbol derived from their ancestral town of Wesel.[9]

The significant role of his great-grandfather in Vesalius's history is quite evident. Vesalius grew up acutely aware of the role Johannes had played in his hometown of Brussels and particularly at the University of Louvain where Johannes fought against the traditions of the past—based as they were in superstition and astrology—in order to redirect the school's medical curriculum toward more terrestrial material knowledge. Vesalius himself would necessarily come to conclude that Johannes's anatomical knowledge was largely erroneous and based in traditional unjustifiable theories; however, he would also see Johannes as a vanguard intellectual who, as demonstrated by his commitment to the betterment of the practice of medicine, believed in the moral responsibility to follow one's own conscience and conviction, regardless of popular opinion. In this sense, Vesalius's own life would come to parallel that of his great-grandfather, not only in his academic achievements and imperial service but in the way that he too forced a shift in the discipline of medicine through a dismissal of accepted and authoritative speculation.

Another of Johannes's important legacies lies in the fact that he established wealth for the Wesele family. As an astute investor, he acquired several properties in and around Brussels over the course of his life and, in so doing, managed to secure his family's prosperity for generations to come. Certainly, in the politics of education, formal academia, and royal service, the legacy left by Johannes was instrumental in guaranteeing that those of his sons and grandsons who wished to pursue an elite education would not be prevented from doing so due to a lack of financial reserve.

Vesalius's grandfather, Everard van Wesele, was the third Wesele to become a physician when he received his medical degree from the very program that his father had helped to establish at Louvain. A scholar in his own right, Everard received recognition for his medical commentaries on the books of Rhazes and on Hippocrates' *Aphorisms*, copies of which Vesalius came to possess and treasure. In fact, Vesalius too would look to the books of Rhazes for his own bachelor's thesis in medicine and his first publication. In keeping with the family tradition, Everard took up service with the family of Mary of Burgundy (the sole heir to the Burgundian kingdom) and her husband, Emperor Maximilian I.

Vesalius's father, Andries van Wesele, was the illegitimate son of Everard. Despite his father's social offense, Andries was nonetheless accepted into the Wesele family home and received nearly the full rights of inheritance of his family name. Although it sounds odd that a "bastard" child would come to be incorporated into the family of his adulterous father, in late fifteenth-century Brussels, it was not uncommon for illegitimate children of noble fathers to be considered patricians as much as the rest of the family. In fact, many illegitimate children became prominent citizens of state and church, successful financiers, and prosperous merchants due to their fathers' recognition. This being said, it does appear that Andries van Wesele's illegitimacy impeded his ability to receive a university degree in medicine like his forefathers; nonetheless, he was formally trained as an apothecary, which did not require a university education. Although an apothecary did not hold the same status and prestige as a physician, Andries was recognized for his expertise and competency when he too was called to assume royal appointments: During his apprenticeship, Andries was personal apothecary to Margaret of Austria and Maximilian. When he became a full master apothecary, Andries assumed the esteemed position of *valet de chambre* to Emperor Charles V of the Habsburg monarchy. In 1532, the emperor declared Andries van Wesele "legitimate" as reward for his loyal and capable service.

Desiring that his son fulfill his familial destiny, Andries ensured that Andreas Vesalius received the prerequisite primary school education—complete with Latin and Greek studies—that would permit him to one day pursue a university medical school degree. With Andries being appointed the status of legitimate son, the opportunity for his own son to receive the university education that he himself had been denied became a certainty. In 1533, Vesalius would live up to his father's expectations and follow in the footsteps of his family name, entering the prestigious University of Paris to study medicine.

Chapter Two

A Man of His Time

LOCATED FIRMLY WITHIN THE EARLY European Renaissance, Vesalius was both witness and player to this age of intellectual development and social upheaval. It is thus illuminating to consider the impact that four defining events of the time—the discovery of the New World, the rise of the Protestant Reformation, the introduction of the humanist educational curriculum, and the advent of the printing press—had on Vesalius's life, worldview, and work.

i. The New World

Between 1492 and 1522, the European worldview changed radically with Christopher Columbus's discovery of North America and Ferdinand Magellan's circumnavigation of the earth. In the early fifteenth century, scholars had translated Ptolemy's second-century text, *Geography*, into Latin, and by 1477, a Latin edition was printed, becoming a popular source of inspiration to geographers, cosmographers, mapmakers, and explorers. Not only did Ptolemy's book introduce a grid of lines and coordinates that could be physically laid over maps to produce uniform geographical representations—the lines of latitude and longitude—but Ptolemy also promoted the notion that discovered "truths" were necessarily tentative and that continued investigation and observation should be pursued in order to establish new and more accurate accounts. Aligned with this position, sixteenth-century scholars in geography and cosmography eagerly awaited reports from European voyages and explorations in order to incorporate new findings into their own work, while academics and intellectuals focused on the ramifications of Ptolemy's epistemological presuppositions.

With each newly discovered region and people, the world and imagination of the European citizenry stretched beyond their immediate understanding, forcing individuals to reflect not only on the nature of these newfound lands but also on their own place and purpose within God's plan. The intellectual atmosphere of the day was one of uncertainty, for the questions that arose from these unknown lands becoming known necessarily inundated the citizenry with exhilaration, awe, doubt, and fear. This spirit of exploration and the breakdown of convention came to infuse all aspects of European culture, economy, and consciousness. The appearance of gold and silver from the Americas, for example, and exotic spices and silks from China and India diversified and bolstered the economies of most European states and generated a demand for a wealth of luxury items and a universal medium of exchange by which to trade them.

The uncommon appearance of previously unknown or unseen peoples also brought with them a taste of unimagined dress, customs, and beliefs. Although the impact of new cultures and new commodities was generally welcome, the fact that their origins were effectively unknown was disorienting for the general European populace whose principal knowledge of the world was limited to their local townships. In 1536, Gerard Mercator, a cartographer, and Gemma Frisius, a physician, mathematician, and school friend of Vesalius, created one of the first terrestrial globes—a spherical map that represented the known land and water masses of the world as they were then believed to be—and effectively established a dramatic change in how people understood their own physical position within a vast and expanding space. Theoretically, through the visual aid of a globe, even common people could position their own location upon a map and thus understand, however abstractly, their physical proximity to the newfound lands and goods of the day. Just as Gemma and Mercator generated a visual representation of the discoveries of recent navigations and explorations, Vesalius would come to reorient the human body by mapping out the anatomical structures discovered through the practice and art of dissection.

ii. Reformation and Humanism

Vesalius was raised, at least formally, within the Catholic Church. Although the Holy Roman Emperor Charles V—for whom Vesalius's father was in service—was known to be a progressive Catholic, the sixteenth-century religious stirrings of the German reformer Martin Luther were not well received by the emperor. As a result, from a very young age, Vesalius was witness to the social uprising and religious dissidence of the Protestant Reformation. Contrary to the Church's staunch insistence that the word of God was its exclusive domain and that escape from damnation was dependant on obedience to Church teachings, the religious Protestant reformers believed that the Bible—as the primary source of all divine knowledge—could and should be read and interpreted by individuals themselves. Protestantism insisted that faith and attention to scripture, not blind reverence to Church dogma, were the true path to personal salvation. The empowerment of the individual was experienced by many as a profound and liberating idea that was able to gain momentum and rational support, in part, because of a compatible and simultaneous shift occurring in the curriculums of educational institutions throughout northern Europe.

One of the intellectual shifts that characterized and animated the late Renaissance was the rediscovery and reexploration of the language, literature, and philosophy of ancient Greece and Rome. Previously abandoned for being void of Christian influence, the works of antiquity returned as secular sources of insight and cultural achievement. Although the Middle Ages are often referred to as a period devoid of enlightenment, hence the term *Dark Ages*, it was in fact within this period that the return of the age of light began. With a growing belief in a common European ethnic heritage, social thought began to direct its attention to its supposed Greek and Latin origins. This scholastic reflection necessarily redirected social life away from a revealed universe mediated by the Church and toward an understanding of a world based on the assumption that human beings, as the pinnacle of all of God's creations, are the best source of inquiry, meaning, and knowledge. This shift brought many intellectuals to emphasize and legitimize critical thought, reason, and classical scholarship as reflective of God's own internal order. Through the fifteenth and sixteenth centuries, the *studia humanitatis*, the study of humanity, became the foundation of what would come to be called *humanism*. In contrast to traditional Aristotelian scholasticism and its emphasis on dialectical logic, the return of liberal arts education was characterized by a curriculum based in the arts, language, literature, and critical inquiry.

Humanist studies fuelled a passionate interest in the secular wisdoms of antiquity, and many scholars traveled far and wide in search of classical manuscripts of this age. For example, many Italian scholars went to Greece in search of unknown works from writers such as Plato, Hippocrates, and Aristotle. At the same time, there was a gradual westward migration of contemporary Greek scholars who, when faced with the decline of Christian Byzantium and the rise of the Turkish empire,[10] left for more hospitable lands, bringing with them a thorough knowledge of the Greek language and a willingness to provide instruction to eager European scholars. Prior to this time, knowledge of the Greek language, even among elite scholars, was rare; thus most Greek works were known only from Latin translations. These renditions, often incomplete and selective, were not translated directly from Greek but were derived from secondary Arabic translations. Fortunately, unlike in the western Europe of the Dark Ages where classical learning was suppressed, Arabic interest in Hellenic philosophy and medicine flourished to the benefit of all who would later seek out these ancient wisdoms.

In the field of medicine, the early sixteenth century saw the impact of humanist scholarship manifest in the reclaiming of ancient medical treatises, particularly those of Hippocrates (fifth century BCE) and Galen (second century CE). Although the elucidations of these men played a role in the practice of medicine throughout the Middle Ages, their ideas had been transmitted through the lens of Arabic authorities and medieval Aristotelian scholasticism. It thus became the work of Renaissance medical scholarship to generate manuscripts that reflected "pure" translations of the Greek originals in hopes of returning them to their rightful glory. Many of Vesalius's intellectual contemporaries, who wished to return medicine to its classical origins, pursued such ends at the expense of grounded empirical evidence that demonstrate contradictory findings but supported alternative medical "truths." It would become Vesalius's life work to oppose the traditionalist scholars in order to reveal to them the "impossible" reality that they had learned to deny.

iii. The Advent of Print

Part of the incredible inheritance that Vesalius received from his family was a collection of medical and philosophical manuscripts belonging to (and in some cases authored by) his great-grandfather, Johannes. For students and scholars alike, gaining access to original or copied texts was a difficult if not impossible task until the early sixteenth century. Although various monastic and secular *scriptorias*, copying studios, produced multiple copies of popular works for public sale, more rare and obscure manuscripts remained relatively inaccessible. The Wesele collection consisted of rare editions that had been manually scripted, a process that was difficult to undertake in terms of locating original texts, receiving permission to copy them, and being able to afford the costly endeavor of copying. On occasion, some manuscripts were made available through private loan or paid library or university services, but more often than not, the process necessitated a scholar or commissioned artisan to travel to the distant location of a desired text and laboriously copy its contents to the best of his skill and character.

Vesalius often reflected on his collection of treasured books with pride and nostalgia, a gesture that clearly speaks to the role that the family library played in the development of his own imagination, scholarship, and medical study. For a man who would become infamous for creating a text as unique in its form as in its content, Vesalius's relationship to the privileged medium of the *text* as a source of both inspiration and education is of no small significance. How serendipitous that such a young scholar, with so much to say and show, should find himself born within an age where the printed word would change the world forever.

The desire of scholars to reclaim original classical manuscripts of the past collided during the fifteenth and sixteenth century with a revolutionary technology that allowed newly translated Greek, Hebrew, and Arabic texts to be made available to a wide-reaching audience.[11] The printing press harnessed the same amount of labor-power as the time-consuming and expensive process of copying texts manually but generated a far greater volume of finished manuscripts in a much shorter time frame and at a fraction of the cost of *scriptoria* production. The significance of this change is made evident in the following example: In 1483, the Ripoli Press in Florence charged three florins per quinterno for setting up and printing Ficino's translation of Plato's *Dialogues*. A scribe might have charged one florin per quinterno for duplicating the same work. The Ripoli Press produced 1,025 copies; the scribe would have turned out one.[12]

Unlike copied manuscripts, which required pages of vellum (calf skin) or parchment (sheep or goat skin), printed editions utilized readily available and inexpensive paper, a change that significantly altered the appearance, feel, and weight of published books. Printing also allowed for the use of formatting features: title pages, paragraphs, subheadings, and chapters were introduced to help structure text and make it easier to read; printers began to experiment with typing and editorial features such as footnotes and graduated types; title pages became increasingly common which facilitated the production of book lists and catalogues and thus acted as a form of advertisement; and hand-drawn illustrations were replaced by more easily duplicated woodcuts and engravings, innovations which eventually helped to revolutionize technical literature by introducing "exactly repeatable pictorial statements" into all kinds of reference works.[13] In essence, print gave printers the opportunity to experiment with print layouts and features that had previously not been possible with hand-copied manuscripts; thus publishers and their authors became known for specific print styles and qualities, particularly if their changes improved the organization of the material or made a book more aesthetically pleasing to its readers.

From the period following the establishment of the first printing press in the 1460s, academics and those interested in scholarly or literary pursuits became exposed to a rapidly expanding wealth of affordable and accessible printed material. By the 1530s, the printed book, as an artifact and medium of communication, had moved from its cradle stage, its *incunabula*, into adolescence. Printing and publishing had become an enterprising industry, bringing not only a dynamic flow of information and communication but also a science of production and profit. Then, as now, the choice of who and what to publish was less an issue of what was worthy to print and more a question of "Will it sell?" To answer this critical question, publishers of Vesalius's day sought direction from the educational institutions.

Unlike the scholastic system of the twelfth and thirteenth centuries, which focused on pious educational leaders who led students through established readings of a few traditional texts, the *studia humanitatis* curriculum encouraged intellectuals and students alike to read and interpret academic and theological writings themselves. The result was that scholastic textbooks were published and distributed broadly to a wide demographic of new readers. With such works being so widely available to students due to mass production, critical discourse, as an emerging societal phenomenon, became increasingly difficult to suppress. For example, as the origins of numerous texts were traced back and traditional translations were compared to their first editions, numerous errors in translation were discovered, discrediting many popular and widely studied editions.[14] The import of this intellectual and cultural movement toward "pure" translation was not simply a matter of setting right what was newly understood to be wrong—it was a reawakening of humanity itself.

> The more Greek texts were unearthed, the more corrupt Latin translations were purified, the more there was a sense of getting closer to the pure well-springs of inspiration, to the pristine origins of all the wisdom that God had initially imparted to man.[15]

Print also allowed scholars to more easily publish and promote their own ideas to a much wider audience. Thus intellectuals across disciplines were, through the advent of print, able to seed intellectual debate beyond the confines of the university and express themselves within the broader public sphere. This historical change is particularly relevant to a following of the accomplishments of Andreas Vesalius, for it must be stated that the ability to create a text and have it reproduced many times over allowed authors to achieve a degree of popularity, celebrity, and immortality previously unimagined. When we understand that nearly all of Aristotle's writings were lost in time and remember how the works of Plato, Hippocrates, and Homer nearly disappeared altogether; when we recognize how many great thinkers will never be known because their writings did not survive, then we see that the occasion of our interest in a man, Andreas Vesalius, and his famous text, the *Fabrica*, is not simply a reflection of a masterful text that must be remembered but of a process that allowed his achievement to be preserved.

CHAPTER THREE

A Man of His Education

CRITICAL TO THE SHAPING OF the scholar and innovative anatomist, the substance of Vesalius's education point to the seeds of his future dissent. In the fifteenth and sixteenth centuries, the appearance of the *studia humanitatis* began to infiltrate many academic institutions. As the future physician studied the ancient wisdoms of Aristotle, Plato, Hippocrates, and Galen, he found in their efforts and in those of his personal mentors a drive to uncover the truths of the natural world and the confidence to stand behind one's beliefs—even in the face of grave opposition.

i. The Brothers of the Common Life

If the youth of today twist uncomfortably at the prospect of learning the three Rs of reading, 'riting, and 'rithmetic, then one can only imagine the misery they would experience if forced to enroll in the Brussels schools of the Brothers of the Common Life. Since opening its doors in 1515, this religious educational community was intended to provide young men born into wealthy professional families with the requisite education for the pursuit of university study. It is believed that Andreas Vesalius entered the Brothers of the Common Life school just months prior to his sixth birthday and remained there from 1520 until 1529.[16] Although details of Vesalius's particular experience at the school are unknown, a brief introduction to the school and its curriculum offers a window into the intellectual stimulation of his youth.

The general curriculum of medieval times and the European Renaissance entailed lessons in the *trivium* of the Latin liberal arts, which was the essential background for all advanced academic and professional study. The Latin term *trivium* literally translates as "place where three roads meet" and refers to the three aspects of the introductory curriculum of a proper medieval education: Latin grammar, rhetoric, and logic. This material was commonly supplemented with studies in arithmetic and language. Although the standard structure of the trivium appears conservative, the Brothers of the Common Life were uniquely progressive relative to Catholic schools. Created in the spirit of the emerging Christian Humanism, a movement particularly popular in Dutch cities like Brussels, Vesalius's earliest education emphasized, at least formally, direct rather than mediated access to religious scripture and authoritative texts. Established by Geert Groote of Deventer, the Brothers of the Common Life followed *devotio moderna,* modern devotion, and advocated for individual, rather than mediated, pious study of Christian scripture as a means of establishing a direct and personal relationship with God. This philosophy was an evolution in thought engendered by the appearance of the printing press and the subsequent mass distribution of printed materials. No longer were sacred texts accessible only to clergy and scholars. With a large and dynamic industry focused on the translation, reproduction, and distribution of religious and classic works, books were, for the first time, being put into the hands of the laity and the masses at large. [17]

Contrary to its official educational mandate, the Brothers of the Common Life nonetheless worked to relay to its students a *preferred* reading of the texts being studied. Although it was founded on the notion of *devotio moderna*, the school's liberal reputation was primarily based in its practice of hiring lay scholars to lead Christian instruction. But in terms of its teaching objective, the school's principal concern was still to introduce "a fixed set of ideas and facts into the pupil,"[18] not to encourage critical or independent reflection. In essence, the nature of this early program of study was to wisely lead the student "in the ordering of experience and the means of giving expression to this knowledge."[19]

ii. The University of Louvain

On February 25, 1530, at the age of fifteen, "Andreas van Wesel de Bruxella" registered at the University of Louvain and took up residence at one of the school's four colleges, the Castle School. The school was located just thirty kilometers east of Brussels. Vesalius's decision to attend the University of Louvain was likely long anticipated. Conveniently located and well-regarded, Louvain was also an important and entrenched part of Vesalius's family history. Johannes van Weselle, Vesalius's great-grandfather, had been instrumental in establishing the University of Louvain's medical school, and Everard, Vesalius's grandfather, had also received his education at the University of Louvain. So had Vesalius's longtime mentor, Nicolas Florenas, who was a family friend and confidant to Vesalius throughout his life. If one recalls that Vesalius's father was not permitted a university education due to his illegitimacy, it becomes all the more salient that Vesalius must have felt compelled to begin his academic career at the nearby university. Although it is not certain that Vesalius yet hoped to attend medical school when he matriculated at Louvain, it appears likely in light of his natural interest in dissection as a child and his fascination with his great-grandfather's medical library. Vesalius, it seems, desired to restore the Wesel family formally to its proper eminence as a family of physicians.

The University of Louvain was, in the words of the sixteenth-century philosopher Lipsius, the "Belgian Athens," a place most "suitable for learned leisure."

> Can a site be healthier or more pleasant? The atmosphere pure and cheerful; the spaces open and delightful; meadows, fields, vines, groves, nay, I may say, a *rus in urbe* [countryside within town]. Ascend and walk round the walls; what do you look down upon? Does not the

wonderful and delightful variety smooth the brow and soothe the mind? You have corn, and apples, and grapes; sheep and oxen; and birds chirping or singing. Now carry your feet or your eyes beyond the walls; there are streamlets, the river meandering along; country—houses, convents, the superb fortress; copses or woods fill up the scene, and spots for simple enjoyment.[20]

In addition to the glory of its scenic views, Louvain had, since its inception in 1425, consistently managed to secure strong financial backing from its municipality. As a result, its faculties were able to compete with more established universities in attracting some of Europe's leading intellectuals. Throughout the fifteenth and sixteenth centuries, the University of Louvain held a coveted reputation as a progressive institution. However, not unlike the Brothers of the Common Life school, its status as a forward-thinking institution was, at least in its early years, not a reflection of its curriculum but of its policy to allow lay faculty to teach religious material.

Modeling itself after the University of Paris, the University of Louvain mandated that students first receive an arts degree before pursuing an advanced degree in theology, medicine, or canon (i.e. civil law). To this end, each of Louvain's four colleges offered separate programs of study for the completion of an arts degree. The Castle School was, according to Vesalius, the university's "leading and most distinguished school" at the time.[21] Though the colleges may have differed in the nature of the education they provided, they used the same method of instruction. Course materials were taught by the *lectio* (lecture) method, which allowed professors to guide their students' understanding of traditional texts by reading them aloud and incorporating their own insightful analyses as they went. Vesalius himself would later reflect on the experience of being a student at the Castle College.

I devoted myself to philosophy. In such commentaries on Aristotle's *De anima* as were read to us by our teacher, a theologian by profession and therefore, like the other instructors at that school, ready to introduce his own pious views into those of the philosophers . . . [22]

Even after printed versions of standard texts became widely available to students, the *lectio* method remained the standard modality in most educational institutions, including the University of Louvain. Supplementary to the standard curriculum, some students worked closely with smaller groups of students and mentoring professors, usually for a fee or favor, in more specialized areas of analysis. But even here, it should be noted, the university remained responsible for the substance of these private lessons and chose the professors who were permitted to teach them.

To explicate more clearly the essence of Vesalius's early education, historians Copenhaver and Schmitt offer a useful overview of the Renaissance curriculum.

> A distinctive trait of philosophical discussion in the Renaissance . . . was that it usually began with reference to some distant authority, some sage of ancient Athens or master of medieval Paris—a Plato or an Aristotle, a Thomas Aquinas or a Duns Scotus. Moreover, many people assumed not only that God had given a single unified truth to humanity in the distant past but also that the remains of Greek philosophy, especially the works of Plato and Aristotle, had preserved part of this original deposit of divine wisdom. Hence it was no surprise and no scandal if an ancient answer to some question was the right one.[23]

The humanism of the Renaissance and its reverence for ancient Greece is here shown as a tautology: If the writings of antiquity are considered closest to divine revelation, then all present-day questions are best answered by the light of the writings of antiquity. It is not clear whether the answers are right and correct in themselves or if they are right and correct because of the source of the answer. Vesalius's education was grounded in Aristotelian scholastic orthodoxy and natural philosophy, which rationalized that the laws of nature and the heavens were the lens by which all other truths could be determined.[24] The intricacy of this approach and its relationship to other requisite areas of academic study is best personified by a fourteenth-century medical teacher and author, Pietro d'Abano, who insisted on the necessity of studying Aristotle's natural philosophy because "it shows the principles of everything."[25]

Since the city of Louvain was known for its tolerance of progressive humanist ideas, many scholars and philosophers took up residence within its walls and helped to shape the intellectual and cultural community at large. Among its most famous residents was the "Prince of Humanists," Desiderius Erasmus, who "dominated the literary world of Europe" in the early 1500s.[26] Introduced to Erasmus in 1502, Louvain soon found its scholarly societies disrupted by his research and theological writings. Highly critical of the Church and the rigidity of medieval scholarship, Erasmus offended the nonreformist sentiments of many of Louvain's elite. For the emerging humanist scholars and resident students, however, this independent thinker was an exciting character driven by conviction and armed with a mastery of the classical languages. So impressive were his influence and insight that his good friend, the humanist scholar and rector of the university, Bishop Adrian of Utrecht (who later became pope), offered him a teaching position at the university. Erasmus had previously lectured at the university on a number of occasions but had declined a full professorship, preferring to remain a free and independent agent. Finding the atmosphere of Louvain stifling, a disenchanted Erasmus left in 1504 after daunting criticisms of his translations and reinterpretations of traditional Greek texts and "sacred" Church writings.

Despite the formal academic curriculum of the University of Louvain, Erasmus and other like-minded faculty and scholars were active in challenging the interpretations of standard academic readings and worked to develop new methodological approaches to their study. As a result, as the years passed and the methods of instruction became more flexible, some differentiation in scholarship could be identified within Louvain's four separate schools. For example, classical languages and literature—the cornerstones of humanistic study—gradually became institutionalized within conservative Louvain through the emergence of two new colleges, the Pedagogium Castri and the Collegium Trilingue. These schools, free and open to all students at Louvain, focused on lessons in Greek, Latin, and Hebrew. At the time, university classes in Greek were ostensibly uncommon; these schools gave Vesalius and his classmates the privilege of being able to read and compare original Greek and Hebrew texts alongside their Latin translations. Additionally, Trilingue studies also emphasized developing a writing style that modeled the clarity and elegance exemplified by the Roman orator and lawyer, Cicero. A serious student of Latin, Vesalius would in later years be criticized for self-indulgence in his extravagant use of the language. As Vesalius's biographer, O'Malley, explains, "It was perhaps in the Pedagogium Trilingue [at the University of Louvain] that Vesalius acquired his considerable fluency—as well as unfortunate verbosity—in Latin."[27]

Vesalius was unquestionably an eager student who not only devoted himself to traditional philosophy but also to the acquisition of newly recovered classical texts, many unknown to earlier generations. In the presentation of such materials, Vesalius came to understand his teachers' courage of conviction as they began incorporating their own firsthand analyses of newly translated texts into the lectures they taught. In effect, these instructors were working to recontextualize traditional and mandated wisdoms in order to facilitate critical discourse on authoritative dogmas and their justifications. One cannot help but suspect how these nonconformists, these voices of dissidence, buttressed Vesalius's own propensity for independent thought and laid out clearly before him the coordinates for his own self-expression and scholastic infamy.

In trying to identify external constitutive forces at work in the making of Andreas Vesalius, part of our argument is made for us when we look to the other ingenious individuals who attended Louvain in Vesalius's time. The student demographic of Louvain consisted of a diverse group of talented individuals; among Vesalius's predecessors and acquaintances, several were destined to make exemplary contributions to the world that they knew and the one that would follow.

Gemma Frisius matriculated at Louvain four years prior to Vesalius's arrival. In 1529, he published a revised edition of Apian's measurement-based

Cosmographicus (or *Cosmographia*), and in 1530, he produced with Gerard Mercator a two-in-one terrestrial and celestial globe. In the pamphlet that accompanied the globe, Gemma provided a brief introduction to basic geography and techniques for using the globe. Also included in this guide was a method by which ships at sea could more accurately determine longitude through the use of highly precise clocks. Governments and private groups alike urgently needed navigational knowledge at the time and offered substantial prizes for anyone who could provide practical solutions. Two hundred years after Gemma's pamphlet was published, the eighteenth-century British clockmaker John Harrison won the British prize for navigation technology with his invention of a chronometer, a precise instrument based on Gemma's theory. Gemma also developed a method of triangulation to produce more accurate mapping of large areas and terrains.

Gemma received his medical license in 1536, a pivotal time in Vesalius's own anatomy studies. His influence on the young physician is evident when one recognizes how Gemma used empirical observations as the basis of his mapping methodology. Vesalius adopted this approach in his study of the human body through the practice of hands-on dissection. Gemma experimented with how best to print labels and legends directly on globes and maps. This is of no small import, since Vesalius's masterwork of 1543, the *Fabrica,* also utilized text and labeling in combination with illustrations and descriptive keys. This form of presentation was one of the first such instances for a medical text—not so in the discipline of cartography.

Gerard Mercator, who became known as the "man who mapped the world," matriculated at the Castle School in the summer of 1530, a few months following Vesalius's graduation. Like Vesalius, Mercator immersed himself in the study of humanist philosophy. In 1544, he was charged with heresy and briefly imprisoned for his Protestant sympathies. Of most significance, Mercator was the first to construct a chart that used parallel lines to represent lines of longitude to coordinate compass work while navigating at sea.

A fellow student at the Castle School, Gerard van Weltwyck, became a distinguished linguist, theologian, and secretary to Charles V. Van

Weltwyck, and he is remembered as "the best Hebrew scholar of his time."[28] Because Hebrew scripture was of great interest to the Lutherans, van Weltwyck became instrumental in mediating the 1540 talks between Catholic and Lutheran representatives. Vesalius would point to van Weltwyck's achievements in herbology in the preface to the *Fabrica*: "Gerard van Veltwyck, secretary to your Majesty and rare example of this age . . . [e]ndowed with wide erudition in many disciplines and tongues he is the most skilled of our people in the knowledge of plants." [29]

Georg Cassander was also at Louvain with Vesalius and became a noted theologian known for liturgical works and his treatises on biblical and ecclesiastical topics. He also worked to promote peace between the Protestants and Catholics. Although no correspondence between Cassander and Vesalius has survived, scholars recognize him as one of Vesalius's close friends who was personally notified of the anatomist's death in 1564.

A scholar at the Louvain's Lily School, Andreas Masius became a noted linguist and student of Near Eastern languages and history. His knowledge of Arabic and Syriac in addition to the classical languages enabled him to play a leading role in humanistic scholarship and contribute to the creation of the Polygot Bible, which contained the Syriac New Testament.[30] Masius was a longtime friend of Vesalius, Cassander, and Mercator.

Anthony Perrenot de Granvelle was probably Vesalius's closest friend. His father had also been in service to Emperor Charles V; after the death of the emperor's grand chancellor, Mercurino de Gattinara, in 1530, Lord de Granvelle became one of two primary counselors to Charles V. Thirteen years later, Vesalius joined his friend in the imperial court where they served together until de Granvelle's death in 1550. De Granvelle's relationship to Vesalius is unique since their lives appear parallel in many respects, particularly in the expectation that each was, in his time, to follow his father's footsteps into imperial service. As we shall see, Vesalius's decision to join the royal court became a key turning point in his life and career.

Whether their contribution was through humanist or theological scholarship, navigation, globe representation, or political or imperial service, collectively, Vesalius's colleagues constituted an influential group of individuals compelled to become central actors in a changing world.

Life in sixteenth-century northern Europe was expanding: outwardly, all known physical limits were being traversed through advances in navigation and missions of exploration; and inwardly, the study of classical languages, philosophy, medicine, and the arts was changing individual identities through a deepening process of reflection and self-awareness. Individual achievements aside, the historical role that Vesalius and his Louvain classmates played was nothing less than the reconstitution of the human being. Contrary to the clearly articulated world of medieval Europe under the Catholic Church, Renaissance humanism took the questions "What is the meaning of life?" and "What is the purpose of man?" and allowed them to remain open-ended. This naturally brought about fervent conflict between those who saw this change as a move toward individual freedom and intellectual liberation, and those who saw it as threatening, fundamentally destabilizing, and above all, immoral.

As Vesalius was completing his arts program at Louvain in 1532, Emperor Charles V declared his father to be "legitimate." It is not clear whether the timing of this gesture was meant to facilitate Vesalius's entrance into the University of Paris's medical school; nonetheless it secured Vesalius's acceptance into the prestigious program. Despite the undoubted wish of Vesalius's father that he enter medical school, it was the influence of Nicolas Florenas, a physician to the emperor and close friend of the van Wesele family, that Vesalius credited for guiding his medical education. In the dedication to his first published work, *Paraphrase on the Ninth Book of Rhazes,* Vesalius expresses his sincere gratitude to Florenas: "When you became aware several years ago that I was going to study medicine you desired to prescribe for me an excellent and useful system for studying the Hippocratic art, which I have followed with the greatest possible diligence."[31]

In a later preface, Vesalius refers to Florenas as "patron of my early studies" and one to whom "I owe whatever erudition or suggestion of such attainments I possess." Florenas was the principle mentor of Vesalius's life, and his import was manifest both in their private correspondence and in Vesalius's most heartfelt dedication: "[A]nyone observing the mutual understanding between us . . . might regard you as my parent rather than my friend."[32] Vesalius's own father was often away from the family home due to his obligations at the royal court, and Florenas's encouragement and guidance appear to have compensated for this absence, playing a determining role in Vesalius's medical career.

iii. The University of Paris

In the summer of 1533, at the age of nineteen, Vesalius took leave of his hometown and traversed the 150 miles that stretched between Brussels and Paris. Following one of the oldest land routes in northern Europe, Vesalius's steps led him past the textile manufacturing towns of Valenciennes and Cambrai and through the fertile fields of the Low Country that supplied food to the expanding populations of the surrounding cities. The road from the north led into Paris, through the rocky hills that had once provided building stones for the Romans, and into the city's sprawling suburbs, *le faubourgs*. Finally, Vesalius arrived at the Porte Saint Martin gates and, having entered, found himself in the area of the city known as *la Ville*, or "the town."

The broad Rue Saint Martin led Vesalius past narrow houses and the grand townhomes that lined the street. Built close together, the hotels were each three or four stories high, with stone facades, slate roofs, and glass-paned windows. As the street opened to the heart of the city, the Ile de la Cité, the city's bustling marketplace swelled with people, carts, and an unprecedented selection of merchandise. A couple of blocks to the right, Vesalius would find the Cemetery of the Innocents, where he would come to spend many hours gathering and studying the bones of its oblivious residents; not far from the river, also to the right of Rue Saint Martin, the Louvre fortress was being rebuilt in an Italianate renaissance style at the king's whim; and close by, construction had begun on a grandiose city hall, the Hotel de Ville. Upon reaching the Seine, the Rue Saint Martin reached the Pont Notre Dame, where an imposing stone bridge crossed the wide river.

A glance to the left, once in the Ile de la Cité, would reveal the towering presence of the Cathedral of Notre Dame; to the right, the halls of government, the Palais de Justice; and everywhere, churches. A few steps across the island and Vesalius would find the Petit Pont, one of two bridges leading to the Left Bank, known as the Université, or the Latin Quarter, where bookstalls lined the streets. To the left, just before the bridge, stood the Hôtel Dieu, the city's largest and oldest charity hospital, dating back to the first century. It was here that the medical students and artists interested in anatomy made their way into the basement to observe the (infrequent) autopsies performed there.

After crossing the Petit Pont and taking an immediate right at the Rue de la Bucherie, Vesalius would find down the narrow street—amidst the houses stretching to the Seine—Paris's Faculty of Medicine. A building near the corner of the Rue des Rats had been home to the Faculty of Medicine since 1470 and remained a rented property until the faculty finally purchased the building in 1486. Another building and garden were added to the original structure between 1513 and 1514, and by 1529, a chapel had been constructed with stained glass windows depicting the Virgin Mary and Saint Luke, the patron saints of physicians, "surrounded by kneeling students."[33] In these modest facilities, students attended lectures and assemblies and lost themselves studying in the faculty library.

As there were no resident halls, students looked for lodgings in the area surrounding the lecture halls. A number of students took rooms with Jean Sturm, who had come to Paris from the University of Louvain around 1529. Although Sturm had moved to Paris to study medicine, he ultimately abandoned this pursuit and began teaching dialectics and logic. A student of Greek and Latin, Sturm had strong humanist leanings and was sympathetic to the writings of religious reformists, particularly the Protestant humanist, Melancthon.

It is not unreasonable to assume that Vesalius was once one of Sturm's tenants due to their shared connection to Louvain, and because Vesalius, in later years, would refer to Sturm as a longtime and esteemed friend.[34] As a well-connected thinker in Paris, Sturm was part of a network of progressive thinkers and medical scholars, among them, Guinter of Andernach, regent doctor at the University of Paris and later one of Vesalius's most influential teachers. The friendship between Guinter and Sturm, who shared a passion for studies in Greek, was likely the means by which Vesalius was first introduced to his future professor.

On September 14, 1533, after having provided documentation confirming his age, nationality, Catholic baptism, and the successful completion of his arts degree from Louvain, Andreas Vesalius was formally accepted as a student into the University of Paris's Faculty of Medicine. Records indicate that on this day, upon receiving full payment of his registration fees, the chief administrator of the school, Dean Jean Vasses of Meaux, affixed his stamp to a certificate officially marking Vesalius as a candidate for the baccalaureate in medicine. Despite the school's mid-September registration period, Vesalius would not begin classes until early November, following the Feast of Saint Luke on October 18.

Although there are not a lot of details surrounding Vesalius's specific years at Paris, C. D. O'Malley offers an overview of the medical school's common course of study.

> Generally, but not always, the first year's courses dealt with those subjects we would call *materia medica*, pharmacy, and physiology; the second, with pharmacy, pathology, and surgery; the third, with physiology, material medica, and pathology; and the fourth, with physiology, surgery, and pathology. A more specific teaching program was assigned to the two professors [in ordinary], which guaranteed that the curriculum would be covered. One year they were required to teach the "natural subjects"—anatomy, physiology and botany—and the "non-natural"—hygiene and regimen. The follow year instruction was given in subjects "contrary to nature"—pathology and therapeutics.[35]

On a day-to-day basis, instruction consisted of two "ordinary lectures," one in the morning and one in the afternoon, each taught by a different faculty professor. Instructors within the Faculty of Medicine consisted of both professors-in-ordinary (full faculty members) and regent professors (affiliates of the faculty, similar to today's contracted graduate student instructors). During Vesalius's studies, Jean Fernel, Guinter of Andernach, and Jacques Froment were the primary professors-in-ordinary. Outside of these courses, regent instructors taught foundations courses that were scheduled for five in the morning during the summer months, and six in the morning through the winter months. The purpose of the medical foundation lectures was to introduce students to the guiding medical principles and texts of Hippocrates, Avicenna, and, of course, Galen, the idolatrized Greek authority on medicine and anatomy. Although these courses were part of the department's program of study, attending students were required to individually pay their regent instructors rather than directing their fees to the medical department.[36]

iv. Patriarch in Paris

In the second century, Galen of Pergamum, Asia Minor (131-201 CE), was perhaps the most revered and prolific thinker of his time. Writing on an extensive variety of subjects, over 350 of his extant works are known today including more than twenty-six treatises on anatomy and physiology. Highly educated and well-read, Galen incorporated many threads of medical and philosophical study into theories that he perceived to be the perfecting of Hippocrates' (460 BCE-370 BCE) theories. Believing that physicians should also be philosophers, Galen rationalized the discipline of medicine through the creation of a systematic framework that incorporated explanations for health and disease with clinical and therapeutic techniques, observational findings derived from experimental research in anatomy and physiology, and other subjects. The sheer volume of his work was monumental, and his explanations spoke authoritatively on every topic he addressed. Galen's impact was so profound and lasting that his theories on medicine provided the framework for Western medical theory and practice until the late seventeenth century. Galen wrote of the importance of his own work:

> I have done as much for medicine as Trajan did for the
> Roman Empire when he built bridges and roads through
> Italy. It is I, and I alone, who have revealed the true path

of medicine. It must be admitted that Hippocrates already staked out this path . . . he prepared the way, but I have made it passable.[37]

Although Galen seemed to believe that his conclusions were infallible, he nonetheless was an adamant proponent of physicians and philosophers learning and discovering truths through firsthand observations and hands-on research, rather than by trusting untested claims from authorities of the past. Vesalius would internalize this mandate so completely that, through his following of Galen's instructions, he would come to undermine the very theories that he looked to verify.

Despite its impact on medical practice, the Galenic system did not remain static over time. Over the centuries, as scholars worked to consolidate the wealth of ideas inherited from antiquity, the application of the theories was expanded and diversified, but in medicine, the core ideas of Hippocrates and Galen retained their integrity.

Galen's work first reached medieval Europe through the philosophical and literary collections of Islamic medical scholars and physicians, who collected and translated Arabic, Greek, Syriac, Sanskrit, and Hebrew texts. Employing their diverse grasp of languages, some Arabic scholars took to gathering and systematizing into one encyclopedic text, a *medical compendia,* the medical knowledge that they had accumulated from various origins. These comprehensive collections and their accompanying commentaries were immediately valued when they finally reached audiences in the Latin West.

In 1514, Henri Estienne, a sixteenth-century printer and publishing innovator, successfully brought into print a limited collection of Galen's treaties translated by the Italian scholar Nicolo Leoniceno of Ferrara. By 1528, various Paris printers were producing Galenic texts and translations at the astounding rate of two editions per month.[38] Just fourteen years following its production of the first Galenic publications, Estienne Press (under the new management of Simon de Colines), published four pocket-sized Galenic volumes intended for a student audience. Published in Latin, these texts included the treaties *De usu partium corporis humani (The*

Use of Parts, a fourteenth-century translation by Nicolas of Reggio); *De motu musculorum (The Movement of Muscles,* translated by Leoniceno); *De facultatibus naturalibus (On the Natural Faculties,* which addressed Galen's theories of physiology, translated by the English scholar Thomas Linacre); and *Introductio sue medicus (Introduction to Medicine,* Guinter's translation and commentary on a Galenic-based work).[39] Guinter, Vesalius's professor at the University of Paris, would prove to be a tour de force in the proliferation of Galenic theory through his 1531 publication of the first nine books of Galen's *De anatomicis administrationibus (Anatomical Procedures),* an anatomical study that had been largely unknown before Guinter's edition.[40] Between 1490 and 1598, close to 660 editions of Galen's medical treaties were published,[41] a figure that reflects both the significance of Galen's work in the fifteenth and sixteenth centuries, as well as the printing industry's capacity to respond to the demands of the marketplace.

Through the 1520s and '30s, the wide and welcomed circulation of Galen's texts and theories raised Galenic thought far above previously recognized medieval Arabic texts and translations within Paris's medical community. Although most traditional Arabic material was still presented by medical scholars, it was increasingly approached only in relation to Galenic material.[42] Galen's growing importance at the University of Paris was evidenced by the Faculty of Medicine's 1526 purchase of the complete Greek edition of Galen's works, published by the famous Aldine Press of Venice, an acquisition that Vesalius would come to benefit from directly just seven years later. Having substituted one form of orthodoxy for another, many Galenic scholars were irrationally committed to the first translated editions of Galen's texts, despite the fact that numerous modifications and corrections were emerging from the Italian anatomists and physicians at Bologna and Padua. These changes to the Galenic texts were not responses to errors of translation or hermeneutical analysis but were critical responses to Galenic assertions that concrete anatomical research had shown to be untrue.

Singer and Rabin[43] offer three explanations as to why Italian scholars were more open to challenging Galen's conclusions than the French:

First, at the University of Paris, the Faculty of Medicine viewed the study of anatomy as a relatively insignificant aspect of surgery, whereas in Italy, anatomy was distinguished as a specific discipline in and of itself. Consequently, Italian anatomy textbooks were not brought into Paris's curriculum. Second, unlike the medical school at Bologna, which had since the fourteenth century facilitated the study of anatomy through cadaver dissection and the use of texts by Mondino de Liuzzi[44] and Alessandro Achillini, Paris did not hold a single public dissection until 1493; and on the rare occasion that one was performed, the event was held discretely in the basement of the Hotel Dieu. Despite the Faculty of Medicine's 1526 appeal to the government[45] to provide a regular supply of cadavers for anatomical study, public dissections remained infrequent in Paris for decades to come. Finally, many of Paris's leading anatomy scholars during the 1520s and 1530s were linguists and philosophers with an intellectual investment in recovering classical texts and restoring them to their original exalted position. As a result, these scholars viewed the work of collecting, studying, and translating Greek texts as a pure and virtuous discipline.

> [These] leaders . . . thought of themselves as being progressive—and they were right. They argued that many of the texts of medieval medicine, and especially those derived from the Arabic, were filled with errors that derived from a misunderstanding or miscopying of the original words of the Greeks, especially Galen and Hippocrates. If one could return to the original sources, understand them correctly, and even add to their number by bringing to light treatises that had remained for centuries unnoticed in Greek manuscripts, then one would have a much clearer and sounder basis for the principles of medicine. Confusion would be swept away through philological exactitude, and one would indeed have brought about a rebirth of medicine. These new standards, enforced throughout medicine through colleges of graduate physicians, would ultimately benefit all mankind.[46]

Intellectual leaders, such as Niccolò Leoniceno, Englishman Thomas Linacre (the founder of the London College of Physicians), and Vesalius's instructors at the University of Paris, Johan Guinter of Andernach and Jacobus Sylvius, were all profoundly committed to the study of languages—particularly Greek—and the meticulous translation of Galenic texts. Although it may seem that tedious attention to antiquated texts was a fruitless exercise in relation to the sound empirical research being performed by many Italian anatomists, it would be wrong to undermine the importance of this type of text-based study. Sincerely committed to the medical arts, these scholars of the past sought to relegitimize medical discourse by the light of the classical Greek teachers who were idealized as conveyers of truth. Galen's work was particularly appealing because—unlike most conventional medieval texts of the day, which were entrenched with convoluted commentary—Galen's discussion was clear and concise. He utilized elementary illustrations to convey his findings, and he provided detailed nomenclature for the body parts he identified. It was easy for medical scholars and physicians to get excited about Galen's work, but not all were interested in opening Galen's writings up to new interpretations or assessing contradictory findings.

Unlike most northern Italian universities of the early sixteenth century, the University of Paris, through its conservatism, delayed its intellectual investment in humanistic inquiry and postponed the medical faculty's adoption of Galenic texts into its curriculum. Nevertheless, by the time Vesalius arrived, many of Paris's more progressive instructors had already begun to incorporate their own private study into the otherwise orthodox curriculum. Faculty members such as Vasses, Tagault, Fernel, and Guinter were enthusiastic proponents of Galen and "aspired to a fuller and more accurate knowledge of Greek medicine than was provided by the medieval textbooks."[47] The historical privilege of being at Paris during this time of academic transition and intellectual dissidence must be viewed as a defining element in Vesalius's personal narrative. The authoritative position of traditional texts was gradually coming under intense scrutiny. Rogue physicians and scholars began to refer to sacrosanct texts as dead letters—dead texts—lifeless relics that were, they claimed, being protected from change by a mandate of normative respect and institutionalized interpretation. As a means of purifying the works of Galen and freeing them from interpretational error and poor translations, humanist physicians advocated an increased emphasis on direct anatomical study. After all, Galen himself was an advocate of this practice. But it is important to be clear: the fundamental assumption of these scholars was that Galen was indeed infallible; thus empirical errors discovered through examinations of the body would point to necessary errors in older *translations* and aid scholars in reconstituting the original theories. In other words, the humanist scholar did not desire to undermine Galen—but to affirm him. In essence, the ideological perpetuation of Galen's theories in the field of medicine was totalizing.

v. The Teachers

What few specific details we know of Vesalius's anatomical instruction at the University of Paris are largely derived from his own writings as presented in the introduction to the *Fabrica*. Vesalius offers the weight of credit in the development of his dissection expertise to himself and insists that he is ultimately "self-taught." Nonetheless, he draws the reader's attention to his two most influential professors at the University of Paris: Jean Guinter of Andernach and Jacobus Sylvius.

The primary responsibility for the instruction of anatomy at Paris belonged to Jean Guinter of Andernach, who, in addition to his teaching obligations, also oversaw the annual public anatomy demonstration presented for the benefit of medical students and faculty. Although Vesalius remembers Guinter fondly as a teacher and as a linguistic scholar, he is less complimentary in his regard for Guinter's technical aptitude for dissection.

> I reverence him on many counts, and in my published writings I have honored him as my teacher, but I wish there may be inflicted on my body, one for one, as many strokes as I have ever seen him attempt to make incisions in the bodies of men or beasts, except at the dinner table.[48]

Dissection expertise aside, Guinter was without question a leading scholar in the Latin translation of classical medical works, particularly the anatomical texts of Galen. His prodigious output of work was facilitated by his unique method of translating material verbally to his secretary, who then transcribed and edited the new renditions for her employer.

Philosophically, Guinter was deeply aligned with Galen in his insistence that knowledge of the body was of critical importance to the practice of medicine. In Guinter's 1531 translation of Galen's *De anatomicis administrationibus,* the logic for this assertion is presented as follows:

> As poles to tents and walls to houses, so are bones to living creatures, for other features naturally take form from them and change with them . . . Since, therefore, the form of the body is assimilated to the bones, to which the nature of the other parts corresponds, I would have you first gain an exact and practical knowledge of human bones. It is not enough to study them casually or read of them only in a book. No, not even in mine . . . though I am persuaded that it excels all earlier works in accuracy, brevity, and lucidity. Make it rather your serious endeavor not only to acquire accurate book-knowledge of each bone but also to examine assiduously with your own eyes the human bones themselves.[49]

As this excerpt reveals, Galen insisted not only on acquiring anatomical knowledge but on gaining knowledge through one's own eyes and, preferably, with one's own hands.

> The student must carefully do everything himself, even to removing the skin. My predecessors actually remain in ignorance of eight muscles, because they left to others the flaying of the apes, as at first I did myself.[50]

The above quotes point to two of the true ironies of sixteenth-century anatomical study: First, Galen unequivocally advocates that physicians should themselves dissect and examine the bodies being investigated, yet this very point would later become a central point of contention among Vesalius's colleagues, when he aligned himself with Galen's philosophy and became a proponent and practitioner of dissection. Second, Galen's dissection of apes became an ideological blind spot for many medieval and Renaissance scholars, who vigorously challenged anyone with the audacity to question whether Galen's knowledge of human anatomy was based on animals rather than humans—a surprising challenge, since Galen himself admitted to not having systematically dissected a complete human cadaver over his career.

Contrary to what one might expect, it was long believed within the universities that dissection was an act beneath the dignity of the esteemed anatomy instructor. It therefore became the task of the barber-surgeon to perform the dirty work. During an anatomy demonstration, the instructor sat high above the barber and cadaver in a chair similar to that of a modern lifeguard post. From his authoritative station, the anatomist would read aloud from a medical text that conveyed standard understandings of what was *theoretically* being laid bare in the demonstration below. At no time did the instructor himself look directly to the body for empirical support for what he was expounding; such an act would be considered superfluous and even heretical: What was known was known, and thus there was no need to seek out supplementary evidence to verify it. To suggest that the wisdoms discovered by those practitioners of antiquity—Hippocrates and Galen— should be subject to further analysis was considered an outrageous offense within the medical community. The study of medicine had, in effect, devolved into a speculative, rather than empirical, art despite Hippocrates' and Galen's own suggestions that knowledge of the body should be derived from firsthand study. Vesalius would later express his disdain and contempt for this theatrical method of dissection, which was practiced not only in Paris but throughout northern Italy as well.

> [T]he vile ritual in the universities by which some perform dissections of the human body while other recite the anatomical information. While the latter in their egregious conceit squawk like jackdaws from their

lofty professorial chairs things they have never done but only memorize from the books of others or see written down, the former are so ignorant of languages that they are unable to explain dissections to an audience and they butcher the things they are meant to demonstrate, following the instructions of a physician who in a haughty manner navigates out of a manual along matters he has never subjected to dissection by hand. And as everything is being thus wrongly taught in the universities and as days pass in silly questions, fewer things are placed before the spectators in all that confusion than a butcher in a market could teach a doctor.[51]

The bitterness with which Vesalius speaks here is in response to the reaction that he received himself when, as a practitioner of the rising humanist values of the day, he followed the advice of the classical authorities and performed dissections himself. The larger medical community perceived this departure from tradition as an act that undermined their profession and violently criticized Vesalius for it. But the excessive nature of their aggression points to a more fundamental issue: Vesalius's critics felt that the classic medical theorists around whom their status and identities revolved were at risk of being challenged and humiliated—thereby debunking their own expertise. How else might one explain that, despite Galen's own thesis that firsthand dissection was essential to anatomical knowledge, proponents of Galen's (ape-based) theories vehemently rejected Vesalius's firsthand anatomical studies of human beings?

Vesalius did not credit his teacher, Guinter, for the dissection skills he acquired while attending the University of Paris, but he was perhaps too quick to undermine Guinter's influence on him altogether. Guinter's strong support of Galen's assertion that the study of anatomy should be done through firsthand dissection was of immeasurable importance to Vesalius's own philosophical foundation. As his own words attest, Guinter was greatly frustrated by those who did not base their knowledge of the body on direct anatomical study.

> How many Rabbins of physicians there are today who
> widely declaim themselves as Hippocratics or Galenists or
> greater than those, and do not even understand the books
> of the anatomists, who have not attended dissections or
> demonstrated them to others. If you withdraw the title
> [of physician] from them, you will find only dispensers of
> syrups and purges, delighting their patient's palates rather
> than curing their diseases.[52]

Guinter expresses his disgust for those medical practitioners who did not understand the craft they purported to know, yet there is little evidence (outside of his own words) to suggest that Guinter physically performed any public dissections himself. Nevertheless, if one thing is clear, it is that he did try to teach in accordance with Galenic principles by offering his students, particularly Vesalius, the opportunity to dissect cadavers themselves whenever possible.

While Vesalius attended the University of Paris, Guinter worked fervently on a practical anatomy handbook for students that would outline a complete and concise summary of Galenic anatomical theory to date. Closely adhering to Galenic anatomical principles, Guinter looked to dissection as a means of confirming and clarifying the material. To this end, Vesalius was asked to assist. In 1536, *Institutionum anatomicarum secundum Galeni sententiam ad candidatos Medicinae libri quatuor* (*Anatomical Institutes according to Galen for Candidates in Medicine in Four Books*) was published. Although Guinter praises Vesalius as "a young man, by Hercules, of great promise, possessing an extraordinary knowledge of medicine, learned in both languages [Latin and Greek], and very skilled in dissection of bodies,"[53] and explicitly gives him credit for assisting him skillfully in the dissection of spermatic vessels, it is generally believed that Vesalius's contribution to the project was significantly more extensive than Guinter's acknowledgements suggest. However inadequate this reference may have been, to be formally recognized by a revered anatomical scholar within a popular and widely distributed anatomical handbook was not a trivial achievement for

Vesalius. It would be an interesting turn, however, when two years following the work's original publication, Vesalius took it upon himself to edit and correct the original edition of Guinter's *Institutiones*. In 1538, the new unauthorized edition was published, and although Guinter was still named as the author of the text, a generous dedication to Vesalius was *added* to the preface.

Guinter may have presented Vesalius with numerous opportunities to work with cadavers; however, it was Jacob Sylvius whom he credits as being a genuinely praiseworthy anatomist. Late to the study of medicine, Sylvius began medical studies while in his fifties and was in the infancy of his medical career when Vesalius came under his tutelage. [54]

While Guinter was known for being a kind and generous instructor, Sylvius was equally well-known for having a less than pleasant disposition— crude, obnoxious, curmudgeonly, and cheap. Some student accounts of his lectures tell of the pleasure he experienced in firing his "three beasts . . . his mule, his cat, and his maid."[55] Another student records how Sylvius once stopped a lecture and refused to continue until his students paid their delinquent fees in full. So stingy was he that it was said that his epitaph read:

> Sylvius lies here, who never gave anything for nothing
> Being dead, he even grieves that you read these lines for
> nothing.[56]

While his students may not have appreciated his frugality or temperament, they could not help but recognize and benefit richly from his organizational skills and instruction in anatomy. As his student Noel du Fail recalls, this too was not without its price.

> I recall having heard the eloquent Jacobus Sylvius lecture
> on Galen's *Use of Parts* to a remarkable audience of
> scholars of all nations; but when he exposed those parts
> which we call shameful, there was no bit or portion he
> did not identify in good French by name and surname,
> adding the appearances and likenesses for the greater
> amplification of his remarks, which would have been

delusive and unpleasant or uninteresting if he had not done so. I have seen him bring in his sleeve, because he lived all his life without a servant, sometimes a thigh or sometimes the arm of one hanged, in order to dissect and anatomize it. They stank so strongly and offensively that some of his auditors would readily have thrown up if they had dared; but the cantankerous fellow with his Picard head would have been so violently incensed, threatening not to return for a week, that everyone kept silent (italics added).[57]

According to Charles Singer, medical scholars of the renaissance had difficulty understanding and synthesizing Galen's works. His extensive yet unstructured adoption of medical and anatomic terminology caused considerable confusion and frustration to an already enigmatic subject. Sylvius directed his life's work in response to this disorientation, culminating in the publication (posthumously in 1555) of *Isogogue*, "a systematic textbook of modified Galenic anatomy, notably superior in its classification of muscles."[58] The sophistication of his achievement was quickly recognized and became "the foundation of modern muscles nomenclature."[59] Sylvius's emphasis on organizing the Galenic language and his hands-on use of dissection as a means of instruction came together in what would be recognized as the most comprehensive and progressive introduction to Galenic anatomy of his time.

Not yet a member of Paris's medical faculty,[60] Sylvius lectured at the College de Tréguier to an audience that was said to have been far larger than those of Paris's professors-in-ordinary. Despite the smell of the rotting objects of study, students, instructors, and commoners alike were drawn to his lectures and dissections. As human cadavers were the property of the university, the dean of medicine allocated what few were available to faculty professors and not to regent instructors. Animal carcasses, on the other hand, were abundantly available; thus all of Sylvius's public dissections were performed on dogs and other animals. Despite this limitation, Vesalius would come to publicly credit Sylvius as being a genuinely credible anatomist.

> [T]his project [the *Fabrica*] would never have gone forward if when I was studying medicine at Paris I had not personally set my hand to Anatomy at a time when my fellow students and I had to content ourselves with a few internal parts being superficially displayed at one or two public dissections by the most ignorant barbers. So perfunctorily was Anatomy treated in the place where we first saw medicine revive, that I myself, trained in a few dissections of animals under the famous and never sufficiently praised Jacob Sylvius, at the urging of friends and instructors conducted a better than usual public dissection—the third anatomy I ever attended.[61]

It is important to point out here that, as frustrated and repeatedly disillusioned as Vesalius was by the incompetent and uninformed instruction that he received throughout his medical training, he repeatedly gave Jacob Sylvius immunity from this criticism. Sylvius, on the other hand, did not offer Vesalius the same exemption in return. Throughout Vesalius's career, as he gathered evidence that contradicted many of Galen's theories, Sylvius became ever more converted to the belief that Galenic *law* was infallible and responded to Vesalius with condemnation—even going so far as to call him an "anti-Galenist" and a "madman."

Vesalius and Sylvius would never come to see eye-to-eye on issues of anatomy; however, the influence of Sylvius as a teacher is important for two reasons: first, Sylvius was a genuine and skilled anatomist whose commitment to the mastery of the techniques of dissection was internalized by the young Vesalius; and second, Sylvius's attention to nomenclature in the instruction of anatomical parts would manifest itself in Vesalius's academic career in his master's thesis and as a key aspect of his most famous illustrated publication.

vi. Extra Credit

The sights of Paris consisted of many attractions for a young student of medicine, not the least of which was the Cemetery of the Innocents. According to Galen, the examination of bones was essential to the study of anatomy, and although human soft tissue samples were rare in the sixteenth century, medical students could acquire skeletal remains with relative ease. As a peripheral discipline within medicine, pre-sixteenth-century anatomy was not allocated many of the tools required to advance its study—human cadavers were not often available for close examination.

Although the study of human anatomy was prominent in ancient Egypt as early as 1600 BCE and adopted by the Greek physicians Herophilos and Erasistratus in Alexandria in the fourth century CE, *speculative* anatomical research would come to be the norm due to Christian and Arabic taboos associated with handling the dead. Just as in the Jewish tradition, Christians ritualized strict burial practices dictating where and how a body must be buried. Christianity's emphasis on laying the body in sacred ground, combined with its dogmatic assertions regarding the resurrection of the dead, necessitated that the bodies of the dead remain intact and uncompromised as they awaited the return of Christ. The practices of autopsy and dissection were viewed as denigrations of God's creation that would later interfere with the body's restoration.[62] In the face of the belief that an individual's salvation hung in the balance, the discipline of anatomical research remained relatively unpracticed until the advent of intellectualism and the establishment of the university in thirteenth-century Europe. Around this same time, in the early 1300s, the Italian physicians Mondino de Liuzzi and Alessandro Achillini reintroduced dissection and public autopsy into practice at the University of Bologna under strict conditions clearly articulated by the religious authorities.

In the late thirteenth and early fourteenth centuries, the political and religious restraints imposed on the practice of dissection and autopsy relaxed significantly, though the practice of dissection remained limited. No longer was the Church the primary dissuader of anatomical study;

instead, public condemnation became the primary obstacle. The Roman Catholic Church did not condemn autopsy or publicly deem its purveyors "immoral"; however, permission from the Church was required before public autopsies could be held. The mediating role of the Church played a strategic function in appeasing the people's social and religious consciences. As Andrea Carlino[63] discusses, formal public dissections gradually emerged as carefully regulated and ritualized affairs, conferring legitimacy on the discipline of dissection. Receiving permission from the religious authorities, who themselves clearly delineated and articulated boundaries around the practice of human dissection, eased the public's anxiety, and the procedures were allowed to continue with ever-decreasing protest. Generally, autopsies and public dissections were justified under the following conditions: first, as a means for physicians and civil authorities to determine the cause of an individual's death, particularly in a case deemed suspicious; second, as a mnemonic aid to help medical students understand and remember the theories presented in their medical texts; and third, as a pedagogical tool for surgeons whose profession required them to acquire hands-on experience prior to performing their trade on the living. Additionally, other practices were deemed permissible but only within an educational context. For example, medical schools could boil body parts in order to clean and preserve the bones for study; however, this process was forbidden to most others, even those wishing to clean the bones of deceased relatives so that their remains could be sent home for burial.

Not only was the practice of dissection limited but *who* could become an object of study was also clearly designated. In most European cities and states, the law required that the bodies used for public dissections were those of executed criminals. It was also preferred that the criminals be of foreign origin, rather than deceased local residents, for the sake of the community. Additionally, "lower class" criminals were necessarily chosen for dissection over members of the "upper class" due to the convenient belief that a person who died by hanging made a better subject for study than one who died from beheading. Unfortunately for the poor, the privilege of being beheaded was bestowed only upon upper-class malefactors. By selecting poor, foreign criminals for dissection, the respectable community at large remained securely unthreatened by the practice of dissection. As a leading pre-Vesalian anatomist, Alessandro Benedetti, noted:

> [O]nly the ignoble, the unknown from foreign parts, can be solicited [for dissection] without affront to the community and to the next-of-kin's known rights . . . There occur in addition ritual purification of their souls and we propitiate their offenses with prayers.[64]

The event of holding mass for dissected individuals appeared as a means of purging the community of guilt. Although the prayers can be seen as an act based in compassion and benevolence, in sociological terms, the community ritual also played a role in justifying the desecration of the body: The dissection became a forced penance bestowed on the criminal's body for the benefit of the community. In return the community bore witness to the reparation and prayed for the soul of the offender, in effect, wiping its collective conscience clean.[65]

Unlike the universities of Italy and Paris, Brusselian institutions remained well embedded in traditionalism. Consequently, the Louvain medical school continued to undermine the value of anatomy within its program, preferring the guiding practices of astronomy to those of dissection. Though relatively advanced in its scholarship of Galen and anatomical study, Paris still found it challenging to supply its medical program with bones and body parts. Because Galen believed that the study of bones was the most fundamental component of anatomical inquiry, students and faculty alike were forced to discretely seek out their own supply of bones for examination. Vesalius would later recall spending "long hours in the Cemetery of the Innocents in Paris turning over bones."[66] Lining the wall of the cemetery, where the "soil was said to strip a corpse of its flesh in nine days," open ossuaries filled with bones made easy pickings for those wishing to collect human remains.[67] But these acquisitions were not without their challenges.

Consistent with contemporary sentiments, grave robbing—the secret means of early human anatomical study—was considered in the fifteenth and sixteenth centuries to be a sacrilegious and sinful act. Even the most progressive thinkers of the day, who understood the educational benefits of dissection, had trouble reconciling the desecration of human remains for profane procedures. Thus the illegal and "immoral" acquisition of bones was necessarily a subversive and even dangerous sport. Vesalius himself recalls being chased by savage dogs while rooting around the royal gallows of Montfaucon,[68] while still others remarked on the monks with crossbows who stood watch over the graveyards at night.[69] The need for extreme caution in the performance of these covert expeditions is reflected in the writings of Felix Plater, a medical student at Montpelier.

> When night came we left the town . . . The two corpses were disinterred, wrapped in our cloaks, and carried on poles . . . as far as the gates of town. We did not dare to rouse the porter . . . so one of us crawled inside through a hole that we discovered under the gate . . . We passed the cadavers through the same opening, and they were pulled through from the inside. We followed in turn, pulling ourselves through on our backs; I remember that I scratched my nose as I went through.[70]

Vesalius too records the fervor with which he and his companions searched and explored the graveyards, the angst of religious prohibitions dwarfed by the thrill of uncovering forbidden knowledge.

> When I first studied the bones with Matthaeus Terminus . . . our supply was very abundant. After we had studied them long and tirelessly we dared at times to wager with our companions that even blindfolded we could for the space of a half-hour identify by touch any bone offered to us. Those of us who wished to learn had to study all the more zealously since there was virtually no help to be had from our teachers in this part of medicine.[71]

The profit of Vesalius's independent study lies in his insistence that he—and he alone—was responsible for the substance of his anatomical achievements and that it was by his own volition that he took to excavating the repressed truths of the dead and challenging the laws and prohibitions that protected them.

Throughout his writing, Vesalius regularly implies that he was all but alone in his practice of dissection at the University of Paris; however, there is some suggestion that this was in fact not the case. For example, the title page of Guinter's 1531 edition of Galen's *Anatomical Procedures* depicts a public anatomy with a number of physicians, distinguishable by their dress, gathered around a cadaver and collectively participating in the dissection. At the head of the cadaver a professorial figure stands—rather than sitting in an elevated chair—and lectures to the audience without a text. This scene stands in marked contrast to the conventional iconography commonly used to depict public anatomies. Whether this image accurately reflects dissections at the time or merely reflects Guinter's philosophy that dissections should be hands-on procedures for all to witness is not known for certain.

More substantial evidence that dissection was not as rare an occurrence as Vesalius stated is present in the figure of Charles Estienne. Beginning in 1531, Estienne is known to have privately performed dissections on human bodies. Additionally, he created anatomical drawings that were much more realistic and detailed than any that had appeared before. Vesalius's own illustrations would be described likewise twelve years later; however, unlike Vesalius, Estienne did not publish his drawings or his research until many years after completing them. Andres Laguna, a fellow student of Estienne, also reports taking up the scalpel at a public anatomy.

> I seized a scalpel and dissected the caecum intestine and clearly demonstrated to all that there were two openings of the same sort, one through which it received and a second through which it expelled, for I had read in Mondino, not so unlearned as barbarous, that the matter was such as I observed it. [72]

Laguna, in 1535, also published a small book on anatomy before returning home to Spain. These few examples indicate that human and animal dissections were not restricted solely to infrequent public demonstrations and that Vesalius's interest in dissection was not the work of one rogue researcher but was, at least tacitly, an accepted practice among anatomists and students of medicine.

vii. Reversal of Fortune

After his third year at Paris, Vesalius and many others, including Guinter, were forced to leave France under the threat of war. In the spring of 1536, the French king, King Francis I, asserted his authority against the Holy Roman Empire through a military push from Savoy to Milan. Holy Roman Emperor Charles V responded to the attack by invading France's most northern and southern borders. The University of Paris's position towards the "impious and inhuman man," Charles V, is clearly voiced in the following passage from the medical faculty's records:

> A great fear possessed everyone as the forces of Flanders, Hainault, and Burgundy and their followers advanced into Picardy where those most criminal of men ravished nuns, despoiled churches, seized several fortresses, and perpetrated many other horrors. They had determined to destroy or at least to sack the city of Paris.[73]

As the threatening Belgium forces from the north amassed along the Flemish border, alarmist voices at the university began to identify Flemish and Low Country students and faculty as "enemy aliens." Rumors of pillaging and threats of violence were successful forms of wartime propaganda that persuaded even the most educated citizens to become irrationally fearful. As the University of Paris's climate of relations became acutely politicized, Vesalius recognized that he would have to leave—not only was he Belgian and thus an "enemy" of France, but his father was the personal apothecary to none other than the emperor himself, a fact that would surely undermine any appeal to neutrality should he have offered it. By summer's end, a frustrated and disappointed Vesalius was forced to take leave of France and return to his home in Brussels with his dreams of receiving a prestigious medical education dashed.

SECTION TWO: THE MADMAN

Must one first smash their ears so that they learn to hear with their eyes?
—Friedrich Nietzsche, *Thus Spake Zarathrustra*

In Nietzsche's *Parable of the Madman*, the prophet from the mountain brought the people a message: "God is dead." In much the same way, section two illustrates how Vesalius came to reveal to the academy of medicine and its esteemed scholars that the patriarchs of their uncompromising commitment and faith were dead and that the anatomical world within which they had been living ceased to exist. Although some were ready for this knowledge and found liberation in its possibility, others deemed it the creation of madness and defamed the young physician at every opportunity. Unwilling and unable to return to the untruths of his early education, Vesalius brought forth a masterfully constructed published work, which revealed to the privileged and lay alike, the interior landscape that lay hidden beneath and behind the blinding authority of centuries of tradition. Despite his success—rather, because of it—Vesalius, at the pinnacle of his career, would find himself in a personal crisis that pitted his destiny against his own freedom in a moment of true "madness."

CHAPTER FOUR

An Unexpected Turn

When Vesalius was forced to leave the University of Paris prematurely in 1536, he had not yet received his bachelor's degree in medicine. Consequently, he would have to return to Louvain in order complete his final year of medical training, marking the first of two defining shifts in Vesalius's life. Terribly distraught and disappointed at having to return to the less prestigious Louvain to complete his medical degree, Vesalius would nonetheless come to find himself richly rewarded for his sacrifice.

i. Heresy in Louvain

It had been only three years since Vesalius had left Louvain to enter the University of Paris, but upon returning, Vesalius soon became aware that much had changed in his absence. With the continued growth of the publishing industry, more and more scholars were identifying with classical writers and forgotten ideals. In essence, theological and intellectual reformers were gaining support and sympathizers—but the stakes were high. The weakening of orthodox religion threatened the Catholic Church, causing an intensified opposition to the Protestant humanist movement by traditionalists. The authorities perceived dissident voices, however innovative or sound, to be dangerous; and for some progressives, the necessity of their words resulted in the ending of their lives.

The Church's prosecution of the English reformer William Tyndale exemplifies the antagonism and hostility in Louvain at that time. Forced into exile for translating the New Testament into English, Tyndale was discovered in Antwerp (a center of publishing and progressive thought at the time) and arrested on charges of heresy. He was then held at Vilvorde Castle near Louvain.

Heresy is derived from the Greek word *heretikos*, meaning "able to choose." Thus, if we take Tyndale's charge literally, the offense in question was that he had introduced choice where before there had been none. By translating the New Testament into English, Tyndale was effectively promoting the ideals of the Protestant Reformation and its insistence that individuals should read scripture themselves as a means of connecting with God and achieving salvation. This was naturally seen as a threat to the Catholic Church, which insisted that grace could only be granted to those who strictly, and without question, adhered to the will of God as made manifest in the canons of the Church. Much of the Church's power was derived from the fact that the Bible had previously been published only in Latin, forcing the largely uneducated laity to rely on the clergy for religious guidance. The publication of the English translation of the Bible meant that many more people could read, interpret, and formulate opinions about its message; thus Tyndale was arrested for providing individuals with the *opportunity* to choose their own devotional path.

The matter of heresy was not simply a matter for the Church, government, or university, as the faculty informally represented Louvain's social and moral acuity. Two professors of theology from the University of Louvain, Jacobus Latomus and Ruard Tapper, led the prosecution of Tyndale and charged that, in translating the Bible into English, Tyndale had "infringed on the imperial decree which forbids anyone to teach that faith alone justifies."[74] Despite being found guilty and sentenced to death, Tyndale remained steadfast in his faith.

> I call on God to record that I have never altered, against the voice of my conscience, one syllable of his Word. Nor would do this day, if all the pleasures, honors, and riches of the earth might be given me.[75]

On October 6, 1536, William Tyndale was strangled and then burned at the stake.

Although Vesalius formally pledged allegiance to the Catholic Church in the preface of each of his publications, there is little evidence to suggest that this was anything more than a political gesture intended to safeguard him from accusations of heterodoxy and keep him in good standing with the Church and emperor. Although there is no record of Vesalius commenting on Tyndale's execution (which occurred just months after his return), his friendships and his own nonconformist leanings suggest he was likely sympathetic to Tyndale's Lutheran affiliation and translation activities. For example, many of Vesalius's friends and mentors, including Jean Sturm and Jean Guinter, were reform-minded individuals who pushed for progressive change within their own disciplines; as a student of languages, Vesalius himself recognized the benefit and necessity of translation as a means of correcting or validating traditional texts; and Vesalius himself was soon to become a controversial and revolutionary character at Louvain for his own challenges to convention and traditionalism. Although Vesalius would not be arrested or executed like Tyndale, his work would be met with violent opposition and professional persecution.

The opposition between the old orthodoxy and new reformists was manifest in all walks of life and in all disciplines of academic study. In 1536, this friction was most palatable within the Faculty of Medicine's heated debate over how best to practice the therapeutic procedure of venesection, otherwise known as bloodletting. Supported and instructed by the writings of Hippocrates, physicians from the age of antiquity through to the nineteenth century believed that illness and disease were caused by an imbalance in the body's natural humoral system: humors beings the body's fluids—blood, phlegm, yellow bile, and black bile. According to humoral theory, an inadequate or excessive flow of humors into an organ, or area of the body, created an imbalance that produced pain, inflammation, and illness. (Emperor Charles V's chronic attacks of gout, for example, were attributed to an excess flow of certain humors to his joints). The physician's task was to diagnose the imbalance and then prescribe a therapeutic regimen, such as bloodletting, that would bring the humors back into balance. It was not long after his arrival in Louvain, much to the resentment of his colleagues, that Vesalius began to address critically the popular discourse surrounding the practice of venesection.

Immediately upon returning to Brussels, the physician of the Countess of Egmont asked Vesalius to attend the autopsy of a young noblewoman who had died at eighteen years of age. It is not known whether this invitation was the result of Vesalius's reputation for being skilled in autopsy or because any student from Paris was seen as an asset to the medical community, but one thing is certain, Vesalius's participation in the autopsy set the stage for a new era of anatomical study at the Louvain and put Vesalius firmly on the path to infamy.

Aside from appearing pale and being short of breath, the deceased female had exhibited no definitive symptoms that would have explained her sudden and premature death. As a result, her uncle, fearing that she had been poisoned, ordered an autopsy. Witnessing the barber's incompetent dissection, Vesalius, a relative amateur himself, took over the proceedings and completed the autopsy—the first autopsy held in Louvain in over eighteen years.

> Following his examination of the body, Vesalius concluded the following: From the constriction of the thorax by a corset the girl had been accustomed to wear so that her waist might appear long and willowy, I judged that the complaint lay in a compression of the torso around the hypochondria and lungs. Although she had suffered from an ailment of the lungs, yet the astonishing compression of the organs in the hypochondria appeared to us to be the cause of her ailment, even though we found nothing that would indicate strangulation of the uterus except some swelling of the ovaries.[76]

It was later recorded that, after Vesalius had presented his findings definitively, the women in attendance removed their corsets as quickly as possible.[77] Although a contemporary reader may judge Vesalius's findings to be amusing—if not ridiculous—they were nonetheless consistent with the medical theories of the day.

Following the initial autopsy, Vesalius and the attending physician had the good fortune to continue to study the woman's body. If the availability of bodies for dissection was limited at the time, young female cadavers were the most rare of specimens. And unlike older subjects, this young woman provided the opportunity for an in-depth study of healthy reproductive organs, particularly the uterus and the hymen. With this unique opportunity, Vesalius began to reap the unexpected benefits of his premature departure from France. This short revisiting of Louvain, it would seem, was to open up for Vesalius, a horizon of possibility that he might have otherwise never been privy to.

ii. Bringing Anatomy Back

Vesalius's entrance into the Louvain medical school evoked a mix of curiosity, resentment, and admiration from both his student and professorial colleagues. His time in Paris had exposed the young medical student to the newest translations of Galen and other Greek physicians; moreover, he had been taught by an elite group of medical scholars and had himself developed skills in the art of dissection to such a degree that he was even publicly praised by the famous Guinter of Anderach for his contribution to the popular anatomy text, *Institutiones*. If we add to this list of accolades the matter of his having performed (immediately upon returning to Louvain) the city's first autopsy in nearly two decades, on the body of a public official's niece, then it becomes ever more salient that Vesalius's presence at Louvain was awe-inspiring and enviously suspicious to both students and faculty alike. Vesalius brought to Louvain, too, another extraordinary advantage—he was in possession of a fully articulated human skeleton.

In the autumn of his return to Louvain, Vesalius's luck and ingenuity brought to him a unique and invaluable learning tool. While searching for bones outside the city gates, Vesalius and his friend, Gemma Frisius, came across the cleaned skeletal remains of an executed criminal.

> I happened upon a dried cadaver . . . The bones were entirely
> bare, held together only by the ligaments alone, and only
> the origin and insertion of the muscles preserved.[78]

After ensuring that no one was witness to their interest, Vesalius and
Gemma worked to remove the skeleton from the stake.

> I climbed the stake and pulled off the femur from the
> hipbone. While tugging at the specimens, the scapulae
> together with the arms and hands also followed, although
> the fingers of one hand, both patellae [kneecaps] and one
> foot were missing.

Although it appeared to the two men that the bones were theirs for
the taking, two problems persisted: first, although the appendages were
relatively easy to remove, the trunk of the body and the skull remained
securely chained to the stake; and second, upon gathering the bones, there
was still the issue of how best to smuggle the skeletal remains through the
city gates and into Vesalius's residence.

> So great was my desire to possess those bones that in the
> middle of the night, alone and in the midst of all those
> corpses, I climbed the stake with considerable effort and
> did not hesitate to snatch away that which I so desired.
> When I had pulled down the bones I carried them some
> distance away and concealed them until the following day
> when I was able to fetch them home bit by bit through
> another gate of the city.[79]

Having illegally stripped the stake of its treasure, Vesalius began the
equally prohibited process of cleaning the bones.

> At first . . . I was unable to cut the ligaments because of
> their extraordinary hardness, and so I attempted to soften
> them in boiling water; finally and secretly I cooked all the
> bones to render them more suitable for my purpose. When
> they had been cleansed I constructed the skeleton . . . With

considerable effort I obtained the missing hand, foot, and two patellae from elsewhere and prepared this skeleton with such speed that I was able to convince everyone that I had brought it from Paris. Thus any suspicion of having made off with the bones was destroyed, although later the burgomaster was so favorably disposed toward the studies of the candidates in medicine that he was willing to grant whatever body was sought from him. He attained no little knowledge of anatomy and was in regular attendance whenever I conducted an anatomy there.[80]

Unable to declare to his Louvain audience that the articulated skeleton was from the remains of one of their own citizens, Vesalius was able to say without suspicion, due to his very recent arrival, that he had acquired the skeleton while in attendance at Paris. That Vesalius possessed such a rare and valued acquisition most certainly suggested to the members of Louvain's medical program—students and professors alike—that he was indeed a man of authority in the field of human anatomy.

Early in the school year, with the support of one of the more progressive thinkers at Louvain, Professor Johannes Armenterianus, and in combination with the liberal offerings presented by the local burgomaster, Adrian of Blehen, Vesalius was permitted to perform anatomy demonstrations at the university, making him, however informally, the university's anatomy instructor. Early records indicate that Vesalius's first anatomical presentation was performed privately within the university. Additional accounts also suggest that the event was not without incident. According to one record, two theologians, waving an antiquated illustration from a well-known medieval encyclopedia, challenged Vesalius on issues related to the "seat of the soul," asserting that he was contradicting one of Aristotle's most fundamental assertions. Although in later years Vesalius would not hesitate to publicly refute appeals to archaic texts or translations, in this instance, perhaps for political reasons or for lack of confidence, Vesalius simply refused to debate the issue.[81]

Interruptions aside, the dissection was deemed a success and resulted in Vesalius's being repeatedly and expectantly invited to continue his anatomy demonstrations before the Louvain medical school.

> [I]n order to do the students at the Academy a good turn and make myself more proficient in a completely unknown subject that was to me of the greatest importance in medicine, I conducted lecture demonstrations of the human fabric—a little more accurately than in Paris—with the result that the younger professors at the Academy are now seen to devote substantial, serious, and diligent work to identifying the parts of the human body, understanding clearly what an extraordinary instrument of philosophy this knowledge provides them.[82]

Vesalius's superior skills of dissection were undoubtedly recognized, but—not one for etiquette in place of intellectual advancement—he inevitably engendered bitter debate with his youthful confidence, experience, and dissident interpretation of classical authoritative texts over the substance of his theories and the extent of his influence.

iii. To Paraphrase

The subject of Vesalius's baccalaureate thesis and first published work in 1537, *A Paraphrase of the Ninth Book of Rhazes*, reflects a combination of interests. The text is a well-intended but amateurish attempt to collapse Arabic (which Vesalius did not know), Greek, and Latin terminology into a comprehensive universal Latin nomenclature. At the time, many of the texts used by physicians and scholars were adopted from various cultural sources, thus creating an inconsistent and multilingual collection of terminology. As a means of resolving this ambiguity, Vesalius attempted to generate a universal Latin-based system of anatomy terminology.

The Renaissance's recovering of Roman, Greek, and Indian scholarship was largely mediated through Arabic and Greek texts. As a result, physicians and scholars—preferring Latin—struggled to find continuity in terminology and anatomical descriptions across translations. Vesalius's thesis was based in the work of Rhazes, born Abū Bakr Muhammad ibn Zakarīya al-Rāzi in 865 ACE. Rhazes was a Persian physician, philosopher, and scholar whose teachings were held in the highest esteem amongst medical academics for many centuries after his death. Despite the continued relevance of this scholar, Vesalius's decision to pursue his writing was not entirely an arbitrary one: First, Vesalius's grandfather, Everard, had himself published commentaries on Rhazes. These century-old texts had been a profound source of inspiration and encouragement to Vesalius in his youth, and they remained his prized possessions throughout much of his life. Second, Jacobus Sylvius, Vesalius's professor at the University of Paris, concentrated much of his study on clarifying and reclassifying Galen's anatomical terminology. Additionally, Sylvius spoke very highly of Rhazes, calling him "the most expert in the art of curing among all the physicians of his people"[83] Understood within this context, the *Paraphrase* appears at once to be the continuation of a family legacy and a means of impressing a revered teacher; yet at the same time, it also marks Vesalius's first scholarly attempt to resolve a problem of his own determining.

It is worth clarifying yet again that the humanist scholarship of the fifteenth and sixteenth centuries was focused on retranslating classical texts, not with the intention of undermining the contributions of the original writers, but as a means of restoring the texts to their original insight through the correction of centuries of mistranslations. The *Paraphrase* thus positions Vesalius's work squarely within this humanist school of thought. He asserts that projects such as his are necessary because:

> [T]he principles of combating disease common to most of the physicians of our time [vary] so much from the methods of the learned Greeks and [remain] so hopelessly and obstinately fixed in the very footprints, so to speak, of barbarians and Arabians.[84]

In explaining the methodology by which he hoped to liberate Rhazes, Vesalius states: "It appeared advisable to me . . . to compare with greater diligence the pertinent works of the Arabians, along with those of the

Greeks" in order to "cleanse" Rhazes' work of translation errors and clothe him "in elegant Latin style." This "cleansing" would allow "the author [Rhazes] himself [to] reach men's hands purged not only of barbarous medicaments and words unknown to Latin ears, but also with his whole discourse improved."[85] Here we see voiced clearly by Vesalius, the humanists' viewpoint—equating the restoration of classical works with a virtuous pursuit. In a gesture that speaks more of youthful arrogance than genuine insight, Vesalius offers that his method of interpretation "did not always attempt to translate literally—which is perhaps expected in a translation—but rather [to paraphrase], adding freely what I judged to be necessary, and explaining in greater detail what seemed to obscure."[86] Having contributed to the improvement of the already masterful original text, Vesalius "humbly" suggests that, if nothing else, his work is an act of altruism that will "liberate other candidates of medicine from immense labour"[87]—a grand gesture for a man of just twenty-three.

With the completion of his thesis, Vesalius received his bachelor's degree in medicine. He was correct in his determination that there was a tremendous demand among physicians and medical scholars for a comprehensive list of anatomical terminology, and his thesis was published immediately. In February of 1537, the *Paraphrase* appeared in print for the first time. Unfortunately, however, the anticipation of the event was considerably undermined by the quality of the book's printing, which was plagued with sloppy typography and broken and worn-out type font. Rutger Rescius of Louvain was the publisher of this first edition of the *Paraphrase*. Rescius was a professor of Greek at the Pedagogium Trilingue, first, and a printer by trade, a far second. Thus, the less-than-auspicious inaugural edition of the *Paraphrase* was likely the result of Rescius's inexperience and a tight deadline.[88] In close consultation with another publisher, Robert Winter of Basel,[89] Vesalius rushed to release a second and far superior edition of the *Paraphrase* in March of 1537, just one month after the release of the first. The second edition was of better quality, and Vesalius had worked diligently to correct many erroneous details that had appeared in the first. The second printing also included the benefit of a subject index at its beginning and was supplemented with new margin notes.[90]

Vesalius would later undermine the substantive value of his first publication, calling it only a "prelude of my studies," but for those interested in following the life of the man, Vesalius's first work reflects his bold ambition, impudent confidence, and exhaustive desire to achieve excellence—a quality that would fuel and mark all of Vesalius's future works.

Chapter Five

Master Vesalius

Comfortable and respected in his position as Professor of Anatomy at Padua, Vesalius took the opportunity to further his anatomical research and participate avidly in the most controversial medical discourses of the day. Although revered by many, Vesalius's list of enemies grew as he became increasingly vocal in his challenges to accepted medical doctrines, particularly those of Galen and Hippocrates. In 1539, an essay on the subject of bloodletting, or venesection, was published, bringing with it violent criticisms and accusations from many in the medical community. What made Vesalius so controversial, so inexcusable, was his insistence on "returning to the body" as a means of substantiating or rebuking institutionalized assumptions, instead of relying on long-held tenets of medical theory.

i. Hitting the Ground Running

At the completion of his baccalaureate work at Louvain, Vesalius redirected his ambitions to a university more able to facilitate his growing professional aspirations. The reputation of the University of Padua's medical program was second to none. The university was established in 1222 as a place of intellectual refuge by a group of students and teachers who had migrated from Bologna to Padua following a dispute between "town and gown."[91] Generously supported, both financially and intellectually, by the governing authorities, the university was liberated from ties to religious ideology, and as such, attracted vanguard intellectuals in search of more provocative and liberal discourse. The school's motto under the Republic, *Universa universis patavina libertas* ("The Freedom of Padova (Padua) is completely for everybody"), reflected the united liberal position between the school and the state. With ecclesiastic concerns decidedly absent from its political vision, the philosophy of the Republic of Venice was simply, and profoundly, that "students follow famous teachers"[92] Therefore the school sought out educated men to provide good governance for the school. This was manifest not only in the senate's funding decisions (for example, liberally supporting the development of Padua's *studium generale* or general stadium), but also in its creation of policies associated with the university's faculty. Fearing that a narrow provincialism in the school's faculty demographic would result in an intellectually limited curriculum and hurt the university's reputation at large, the senate restricted the number of faculty positions that could be allocated to the local citizenry in order to diversify the university's faculty and broaden their curriculums.

Despite its distinguished history, Padua was not without its troubles. Located in the north of Italy, Padua was seen as a strategic military position, and as such, it was often the center of war and conflict. On numerous occasions during the thirteenth, sixteenth, and nineteenth centuries, classes were cancelled, and the school's doors were shut for extended periods. The most significant issue for Padua was the growing Republic of Venice, expanded from the lagoons at the head of the Adriatic Sea, which eventually became the wealthiest power of the eastern Mediterranean throughout the fourteenth and fifteenth centuries. Through the might of its navy and the exploitation of its expansive trading connections, Venice took over much of northern Italy, including Padua, which was twenty-five miles south. The threat of continued expansion brought conflicts between Venice and the League of Cambrai—the allied forces of Emperor Maximilian I, King Louis XII of France, King Ferdinand of Aragon, and others who coveted the Italian territories. Eventually, Venice was forced to make concessions in order to end the conflicts and secure its diminishing republic. The University of Padua remained under Venetian control and was eventually restored to its former glory. The privileges and freedoms bestowed upon Padua reflected life under the Republic of Venice in general and its affiliation with the city of Venice.

> [Venice] was respected and envied beyond all the cities of Europe—famed alike for her wealth, her beauty, her good government and a system of justice which gave impartial protection to rich and poor, aristocrat and artisan, Venetian and foreigner; for, in theory at any rate and for the most part in practice too, every man living beneath the banner of St. Mark was equal in the sign of the law.[93]

Although Padua's liberties were certainly comparable to those of Venice, significant differences between the two cities remained. Unlike Venice and its extravagant Byzantine architecture, water canals, dense foreign populations, artisans, merchants, printers, and bustling market centers endowed with exotic collections of cloth and spice, Padua was notable for the history and prestige of its university and intellectual life. Padua was a modest but hospitable city with many bridges, communal plazas, and arcaded streets that protected its citizens from the summer's hot sun and the winter's rain, frost, and snow. Not without its own prestigious expressions, the city was generously endowed with grand artistry, such as Giotto's frescoes in the Arena Chapel, Donatello's equestrian statue, frescoes by Mantegna, and Falconetto's famous engraved door at the Venetian governor's palazzo. In the truest sense of the expression, Padua was a university town. When Vesalius arrived in Padua in 1537, its population was approximately three hundred thousand with over 1,300 of its citizens enrolled at the university, a significant number for the time. The school of medicine in particular was of formidable size and boasted a faculty of fourteen members, specifically:

> 2 ordinary and 3 extraordinary professors of medical theory, 2 ordinary and 3 extraordinary professors of medical practice, 2 professors who taught Avicenna (also considered medical theory), . . . a professorship of surgery, which later became anatomy . . . , and a professorship of medical botany.[94]

With the advent of the printing press, Padua's faculty became quickly recognized for its scholastic texts in medicine and anatomy, many of which were published in Venice. It is thus not difficult to surmise how Vesalius's ambition drew him to a medical program that promised to introduce him to leaders in the field of anatomical study, while also positioning him strategically within the bold expansion of the Venetian publishing industry.

The University of Padua—unlike the schools previously attended by Vesalius—emphasized anatomical study and introduced specific courses in medical botany and clinical practice. For example, students were required to spend time tending the sick under the tutelage of teaching physicians before taking their final medical examinations. Vesalius himself later recalled the experience of "treating the sick in Venice under the direction of the most famous professor there, Giambattista Da Monte." [95] Padua's regular and frequent dissection demonstrations, maintained for over two centuries, were of great interest to Vesalius.

Having already demonstrated to the medical faculty a superior understanding of medicine and advanced skills in dissection, Vesalius was permitted to challenge the medical program's course requirements and move directly to his intensive final exams shortly after entering the program. On the morning of December 1, 1537, just months after his arrival in Padua, Vesalius began his final examinations before the dean of medicine and Padua's faculty examiners. The medical assessments were held under both private and public consultation over the course of five days. During this period of exhaustive questioning, Vesalius's examiners rigorously scrutinized his knowledge of a variety of medical subjects and authoritative texts. In judging the success of his exams, not only can it be said that Vesalius was unanimously approved for his doctorate degree, but also that, immediately following his last examination on December 5, the distinguished doctor of medicine Francesco Frigimelica, on behalf of his colleagues and himself, granted Vesalius the insignia of the faculty.[96] Just twenty-five days shy of his twenty-third birthday, Doctor Andreas Vesalius of Brussels assumed the position of *explicator chirurgiae,* professor of surgery, within the Faculty of Medicine. Vesalius's teaching responsibilities began immediately, and on December 6, the day following the end of his exams, Vesalius performed Padua's winter-term public anatomy demonstration.

The object of the year's winter dissection was an eighteen-year-old male "of excellent constitution without any abnormalities."[97] For the purpose of comparison and clarification, Vesalius's demonstration included a dissected dog within which he pointed out similar anatomical structures that were difficult to illustrate in the human body. Keeping with tradition, Vesalius dissected the body in the standardized Mondino order (beginning with the abdominal cavity, followed by the thorax, head, neck, brain, and then the extremities) as outlined in the 1314 text, *Anathomia*. But, as a student in the audience, Vitus Tritonius, would recall, Vesalius referred his students, not to Mondino's text but to the explanations of Galen as articulated in Guinter's *Institutiones*,[98] the book that he himself had substantially contributed to.

In addition to the physical dissection and text references, Vesalius also introduced pictorial charts to help guide his audience. A general sketching of Vesalius's original charts, represented in Vitus Tritonius's notes, depicts the gall bladder with the hepatic and cystic duct; the liver with the upper vena cava and branches; the heart and a section of the aorta; and a group of nerves and branches. Tritonius remarked that Vesalius's drawings were somewhat inexact because, the audience was told, the professor planned to publish detailed illustrations soon.

> It is to be hoped that we shall be aided by those illustrations
> which may perhaps be published, containing depictions of
> the nerves, veins, and arteries of the body.[99]

These illustrations would become the subject of Vesalius's second publication, *Tabulae anatomicae* (*Anatomical Charts*).

The occasion of his first formal dissection at Padua appeared to Vesalius as the perfect opportunity to explore a particular interest of his: the proper procedure for venesection. Previously, Vesalius's theories on the subject had been met with contentious debate, but now, as a full doctor and professor at the prestigious University of Padua, he was at full liberty to explain and *demonstrate* his position. The venesection debate will be addressed in greater detail later, but for now it is enough to say that it was as hotly a contested practice at Padua as it had been in Louvain. Diligently laboring over his dissection and explanation of the body's various blood vessels, Vesalius held concurrent lectures on treating inflammation through bloodletting.

The degree of detail and attention that he gave to this subject is reflected in the fact that, despite the astounding two-and-a-half week period over which the autopsy was held, there was not enough time left for him to demonstrate the muscles of the arms and legs. On the final day of demonstrations, December 24, the body had decomposed past the point of its use, leaving Vesalius to recommend to his students that they review the work of Galen in order to cover those areas neglected by the anatomy. With the dissection series complete, Vesalius carefully took to cleaning the bones and articulating the skeleton for future use. It would serve as a convenient model in the production of the *Tabulae*.

ii. It's Just as I Remember

From the cave paintings of Lascaux to the votive figures of Mesopotamia, from the stylized paintings of Egyptian tombs to the sculptures of Michelangelo, the human body has been represented in a myriad of forms with a variety of intentions. In the study of anatomy, however, the golden age of the Greek and Roman empires of the fourth century BCE draw the most attention. In the art and culture of the Greeks and Romans, extensive attention was focused on the external anatomical features of the human body. Awe-inspiring reliefs, sculptures, and paintings depicted idealized human figures in various states of work, competition, and war. With the return to the texts of antiquity, it is of little surprise that one of the defining qualities of the Renaissance was its revitalization of realist artistic representation and aestheticism, particularly in relation to studies of the human body. Leon Battista Alberti's treatise, *On Painting,* published in 1435, spoke to this idea and advocated that artists commit themselves to the task of objectively imitating nature.

> [J]ust as one cannot build a ship without knowing the
> constituent parts that go into building it, the artist cannot

paint the visible human form, without understanding the invisible form beneath it. [100]

Other artists and sculptors of the time, such as Lorenzo Ghiberti (1378-1455) and Benvenuto Cellini (1500-1571), emphasized the necessity of understanding the "bony components of the bodily machine." Many artists ardently took to the study of anatomy and attended public dissections as part of their training. The benefits of this study are nowhere more celebrated than in the extraordinary works of Albrecht Durer (1471-1528), Leonardo da Vinci (1452-1519), Michelangelo (1475-1564), and Raphael Sanzio (1483-1520).

Despite these representational advancements within artistic circles, the adoption of realistic illustration in medical and scientific texts continued to be overlooked as a medium for relaying anatomical knowledge. Although some classical Greek, Roman, Arabic, and medieval medical texts utilized diagrams and schematic drawings, most illustrations were speculative in nature or based on animal dissections. Prior to the Renaissance, the study of medicine had little use for anatomy, much less anatomical illustrations.

In the pre-Renaissance era, the written form was predominantly considered the purest form of representation. And, just as the authority of the written text was based in the notion that the sacredness of knowledge should remain based in written texts and not be corrupted by such a crude and superfluous medium as illustration, "[t]he body was the book which was to be read," and "the real body itself was the true illustration."[101] The body, however, was not a text for just anyone to read. Since it was believed that all the mysteries of the body had already been clearly articulated by the ancient Greek and Arabic masters of anatomy, the physical body too, like its image, was understood to be a gratuitous means of understanding the body. As convoluted and tautological a way of thinking as this may be, the truth and sanctity of classical wisdoms were considered self-evident and incontestable. Thus the study of anatomy and the performance of dissections were seen in most places—with the exception of a few Italian universities—as acts of degradation and blasphemy. Aligned with this understanding, scholars used anatomical illustrations only occasionally, adopting them as secondary mnemonic aids but not as instrumental supplementary guides to text.

It would not be until the sixteenth century, when the weight of humanist intellectual curiosity began to wear at the religious prohibition against dissection, that objective inquiry and representation of the body would return as an integral and meaningful intellectual pursuit. Published in Venice in 1492, the *Fasciculus medicinae* (*Bundle of Medical Treatises*), was the first modern medical text to include illustrations. A collection of six independent medical treatises dealing with various topics including astrology, venesection, women's physiology, and the plague, the *Fasciculus* also included ten full-page woodcut prints, including depictions of an anatomy scene, a pregnant woman, and the venous system. In retrospect, the achievement of the authors of the *Fasciculus medicinae* and its publisher was that they attempted to use illustration to independently portray anatomical aspects of the human body.

Berengario da Carpi's 1521 text, *Commentaria* (*Commentary*), was the first anatomy treatise published with drawings that were intended to supplement the information detailed in the manuscript. At just under one thousand pages, the *Commentaria* was presented as a commentary on Mondino's anatomy text, but in its substance, it constituted an original treatise that exhaustively surveyed ancient and modern anatomy authorities in relation to practical research in dissection and autopsy. Berengario insisted that a good anatomist should be familiar with the teachings of the classical authorities and the work of modern anatomists; to this end, the *Commentaria* references more than one hundred scholars, earning it the reputation as one of the most comprehensive guides to early anatomical literature.[102] Berengario also believed that if one followed the historical sequence of anatomical ideas, one would, through the determining process of dissection, be better able to identify sources of errors as they arose.[103] When traditional authorities contradicted one another in their theories or when texts appeared to have been corrupted, dissection and observation, Berengario argued, could guide the anatomist to a reasonable and verifiable finding. "And in this discipline nothing is to be believed that is acquired either through the spoken voice or through writing since what is required is *seeing* and *touching*."[104] Although history locates Berengario soundly within the Galenic tradition, Vesalius's biographer, C. D. O'Malley identifies him as essentially "the first man not constantly overwhelmed by earlier authorities, either Galenic or Moslem."[105]

Berengario conceived of the *Commentaria* as a practical book based on a practical anatomy of visible things; thus he provided twenty graphic figures illustrating particular anatomical features. As a connoisseur of fine painting and sculpture, who had resided in both Rome and Florence where many of the works of Leonardo, Michelangelo, and Raphael were on display, Berengario had a strong affinity for the visual arts and the role that anatomy played in its subject matter. Although the twenty figures of the *Commentaria* are of mixed quality, collectively, the material far surpassed anything previously seen at the time. The adoption of illustration to reflect how anatomical structures appear before the eyes was an important step in the development of artistic representation as a pedagogical tool within the field of medicine. Vesalius's *Fabrica*, however, would come to achieve something fundamentally transcendent in relation to Berengario's vision.

Vesalius understood early in his education the utility of illustration. While at Louvain, and even more extensively at Padua, Vesalius adopted visual props while acting as butcher and lecturer during his dissections. Illustrations, charts, dissected animals, and an articulated skeleton were used to supplement the main dissection in order to more clearly demonstrate the marvels of the human body. Recognizing the need for and benefit of visual aids and diagrams to more adequately educate students led Vesalius to the subject of his second publication, *Tabulae anatomicae sex* (*The Six Anatomical Tables*). Vesalius compiled six full-page anatomical illustrations consisting of refined renditions of the drawings he designed for autopsy demonstrations. Unlike past anatomical publications, the *Tabulae* consisted almost entirely of comprehensive drawings of the body accompanied by very little text. Vesalius was among the first to make such sheets available to help students learn and memorize what they had observed in the anatomy demonstrations, but it should be noted that they still were not intended as texts for *primary* learning.

In the introduction to the April 1538 publication of *Tabulae anatomicae*, Vesalius articulates the text's objective and utility.

> Not long since . . . when appointed at Padua for the course of the Surgical part of Medicine, in discussing the treatment of Inflammation, I had . . . made a drawing of the veins . . . [which] so pleased the professors and students of medicine that they pressed me for a similar delineation of the arteries and nerves. Since the conduct of dissections was part of my duty, and knowing this kind of drawing to be very useful to those attending the demonstrations, I had to accede to this request. Nevertheless I am convinced that it is very hard—nay, futile and impossible—to obtain real anatomical . . . knowledge from mere figures . . . though no one will deny them to be capital aids to memory.[106]

Today, it is difficult to imagine an informative and comprehensive description of anatomical systems without the use of well-articulated supplemental diagrams, yet Vesalius's introduction makes clear that illustration was considered useful merely as a mnemonic device rather than an explanatory source. The difference is naturally an ideological one: if it was not possible for an illustration to represent the "real" body, then the suggestion that a diagram could somehow make something clearer about the body would necessarily suggest that the represented image had supremacy over the thing itself. Therefore, drawings and diagrams had to be situated clearly as "capital aids to memory" and nothing more. It is not known how philosophical Vesalius was on this debate over illustration and representation; what *is* known is that the production of the *Tabulae* was intended for his medical students, supporting the suggestion that it was intended mainly for supplementary use.

Vesalius was very critical of the poverty of his own formal anatomy education and was adamant in his goal of trying to remedy such deficiencies in his student's education. As Vesalius was particularly dissatisfied with the ineffective dissections that he had witnessed at Louvain and Paris, the use of diagrams appeared as an essential method of relaying accurate and comprehensible information to his ill-informed audiences.

It has been the intention of much of the preceding discussions to map out for the reader the making of Andreas Vesalius in relation to the places and times of his life, education, and family. Although Vesalius demonstrated throughout his life a natural curiosity for the study of anatomy and a propensity for dissection that speaks to a very liberal, if not secular, conscience, it was not until the publication of the *Tabulae* that he appeared a man wholly unique in his field. The significance of the *Tabulae* can be addressed at three levels: the form of its presentation, the anatomical content it conveys, and the success of its publication.

Part of the *Tabulae*'s immediate aesthetic appeal was that it was composed of uncommonly large sheets of paper printed from carefully articulated woodcut blocks. Unique among illustrated medical texts—what few that existed—was that each of the *Tabulae*'s pages, measuring nineteen inches by thirteen and a half inches—featured one large drawing, rather than several small ones. The effect was the creation of a very clear and detailed image of notable size. These pages, the "largest ever prepared at Venice for any printed book,"[107] allowed for more detailed illustration and were large enough that they could be pinned or held up before a class and used as visual references. Vesalius was the draftsman of the first three of the six illustrations presented in the text, while Johannes Stephanus of Calcar, a Flemmish artist and student of the Titian school, developed—under Vesalius's strict direction—the final three images. Vesalius's three plates consist of very stylized depictions of the arterial and vascular systems, subjects of particular interest, as they related to the practice and debate surrounding venesection. Table I details the liver (the "workshop of sanguification"); Table II articulates the vascular system; and Table III details the arterial system. The last three plates of the *Tabulae* consist of realistic three-dimensional depictions of a human skeleton, modeled from the articulated skeleton prepared from Vesalius's December dissection at Padua. It is here that the text becomes something truly special. The three drawings feature the skeletal form from the front, side, and back, as was the custom of medical skeletal illustrations at the time; however, the degree of detail and realism demonstrated in Stephanus's renderings give the skeletons an animated appearance, generating an exciting and compelling confrontation of "reality portrayed from life."[108] The striking dissimilarities between Vesalius's skeletal images and those appearing in Berengario's text from just a few years earlier demonstrate a significant advancement in artistic technique and a move towards realism put forth by Stephen van Calcar's skills and forced into being by Vesalius's vision.

In relation to today's standards, the illustrations of the *Tabulae* appear flawed in many respects and artistically marginal, but art historian Martin Kemp reminds the contemporary viewer to "understand each image in terms of the context of its own generation."[109]

> A representation is made to serve one or more specific functions in particular circumstances and involves a series of choices that reflect the values and priorities of the makers of the image and its intended viewers.[110]

Therefore, if the task at hand is to understand not only the impact of the work but also the achievement of its author, then the task of undertaking is to "work towards a reconstruction of the original 'message' of the images in terms of functions, intention, and contemporary reception."[111] The *Tabulae* represented a concerted effort, first, to create a functional tool for educating those interested in anatomy; second, to demonstrate through clear illustrations the substance of Galenic theories; and third, to correct and modify errors of Galenic anatomical theory as made evident to Vesalius through firsthand observations and dissections.

The *Tabulae* was an instant publishing success and a must-have for medical students, professors, and members of the general public whose imagination had been captured by open anatomy demonstrations and the visual appeal of the illustrated sheets. Emperor Charles V was also a recipient of the text. Although Vesalius had not dedicated the text to the emperor, a common courtesy of the time, he nonetheless asked his father to present a copy to him, who in return, kindly received it. Vesalius's old friend and mentor, Nicolas Florenas, would later write to Vesalius and express in great detail the emperor's praise of the work.[112]

Due to a demand that far exceeded the original limited distribution of the *Tabulae*, Vesalius was forced to endure the creation and distribution of "fugitive" copies of his text, which spread across Europe within a year following its original release. Of particular offense was that these pirated editions were produced with alterations and were of much poorer quality with a less sophisticated attention to detail. Since the new publishers was not required to seek permission from the author or original printer, the only limit recognized in the production of the new editions was that they be of a quality that would satisfy a relatively uninformed market. Despite Vesalius's acquisition of "privileges" from the papal and Venetian authorities[113]—a yet ineffective form of protective publishing licensing— various plagiarisms of Vesalius's anatomical charts began to appear. The first pirated edition was published in Augsburg, Germany, in June 1539 by Jobst de Necker, and was to his credit a near exact copy of the original, but with German text. The quality of this new edition did nothing to soothe Vesalius's resentment, particularly because the unqualified author dared to change the original preface with, as Vesalius described it:

> the preface of a German babbler, who, unworthily decrying Avicenna and the Arabic authors, ranks me with the abridged Galens and, to cheat the buyer, pretends that I have put into six tables what in Galen fills thirty books . . . Moreover, he affirms that in his German translation he has used Greek and Latin terms, whereas he has not only suppressed these but has likewise omitted all that he could not translate and nearly all that gave value to my Tables; to say nothing of his wretched copies of the Venetian prints.[114]

Later that same year, another fugitive edition appeared in Cologne; however, this edition was unique in that in consisted of seven, not six, illustrations. By a strange turn, the additional image was based on a previously unpublished Vesalius chart that he had "roughly sketched for one or two friends who had requested it."[115] According to Vesalius, the plagiarized sketch was "deplorably copied." Although each of these rogue editions was unwelcome to Vesalius, none were as enraging as Walter Ryff's 1541 Strasbourg edition, which not only reworked the content of the text but also did not credit Vesalius as the text's original author. Known for his expropriation of others' scholarly work, Leonard Fuchs, a contemporary of Vesalius's, said that Ryff was "of all men the sun hath seen, the most shameless."[116] Vesalius would heed the lessons of this, his second publication, when presenting to the world his magnum opus, the *Fabrica*.

History would come to know Vesalius for challenging Galenic law; however, this achievement was not yet evident in the *Tabulae*, with one exception: Vesalius notes that the human jaw consists of one—not two— bones, a clear and accurate correction of Galenic theory. Naturally, Vesalius attributes this mistake not to Galen himself but to errors in the translation of Galen's texts over the centuries. Vesalius further locates himself firmly in the Galen tradition when, in the preface to the *Tabulae*, he defends the content of the work by stating that what his audience sees presented in the illustrations is what he had demonstrated to many Paduan students and professors through autopsy over the course of the previous year.

Vesalius's words—his powerful and convincing rhetoric—ring with authority, but the "air of total conviction"[117] transmitted through this exceptional work did not translate into an accurate presentation of the human body despite his having observed reality with his own eyes. For example, there does not exist in human or other vertebrate animals a flower-like, five-lobed liver as is depicted in Figure I, nor is the human spine straight as in Figure V—it is curved. Vesalius's commitment to the conventional anatomical knowledge of the period is also made evident in his representation of the *rete mirable*.

Galenic anatomy suggested that the *rete mirabile*, a network of blood vessels into which the carotid arteries divide at the base of the brain, was where "vital spirit" was converted to "animal spirit" before being sent through the nerves to the rest of the body. In 1326, the anatomist Beregario explicitly challenged Galenic dogma when he denied the existence of the *rete mirabile* after having failed in numerous efforts to identify it empirically. The debate over its existence continued into the 1800s, but in the early 1500s, Nicolò Massa, a contemporary of Vesalius, claimed to have demonstrated the structure many times, though he admitted that it decomposed quickly after death and was thus difficult to see. We now understand that this structure does not exist in human beings; therefore, it is unclear what the source of Vesalius's illustration was: Was it a copy of another scholar's depiction? Was it based on a structure found in an animal? Was it a creation of his imagination, fueled by competition? Or did Vesalius truly believe that he saw such a structure in the human body? This last possibility is not as ridiculous as it may seem, for the power of pervasive theories shapes not only what one knows but also what one sees, even in the light of contradictory evidence.

Further evidence of Vesalius's radical errors of observation (or belief) can be seen in his persistent inclusion of anatomical features characteristic of animals, not human beings. Since Galen derived much of his anatomical knowledge from animals, it is not surprising to find in the *Tabulae*, for example, aspects of the heart and vessels that resemble those of monkeys and apes. These failings were of course not unique to Vesalius's work, as other anatomists including Berengario, Dryander, Estienne, and Fallopio, similarly depicted many of the same animal-based anatomical structures.[118] Again, what is interesting is that Vesalius purported to derive his anatomical knowledge from studying the objects with his own eyes. His errors suggest that traditional medical beliefs altered his visual perception of the world with astounding force. Despite Vesalius's experience in dissection, he is shown here to be very much a man of his time, immersed in the noise of Galenic theory.

To understand the strength of ideological limits and how the *Tabulae* traversed them (at least in relation to the medium of illustration and representation), one must understand something about the structure of authority. Simply, *authority is what authority does*: authority becomes authoritative by and through the very event of its propositions being taken to be true. Understood in this way, the appearance and authoritative success of the *Tabulae* indicates a radical shift towards the supplanting of non-representable truths. This is the revolution of the *Tablulae*. Vesalius grounds the work's authority, not on the truth of Galen, but on the certainty of empirical anatomical research. Although the text still supports Galenic theories, and thus supports the viewers' belief in these theories, the text justifies their truth by stating that *objective inquiry* has proven Galen to be correct. Thus, ideological dissent appears in the form of descriptive illustrations that turn the audience's attention away from speculation and self-evident referencing and toward something *visual*. An illustration, being a form of abstraction, may not represent reality any more or less accurately than a textual or verbal explanation;[119] however, in directing the reader's own analysis back and forth, from text to illustration, it first, establishes—however tacitly—the contingent relationship between text and image; second, makes the reader active and thus complicit in the research of identifying and understanding anatomical structures; and third, logically demands that any challenges to the content of the material be *visually* demonstrated, not simply addressed.

The achievement of the *Tabulae*, though certainly a transitional piece prone to Galenic sympathies, was not in its expressed purpose as a supplementary visual aid, as Vesalius suggests, but in its redirection of the readers' attention away from speculative explanations and toward the suggestion of empirically based evidence. At the close of the preface, Vesalius states that if the *Tabulae* proves to be a successful endeavor, then he will "someday do something greater than this." This statement is remarkable for two reasons: first, it indicates that Vesalius is aware that there is something "great" or ingenious about the *Tabulae*; and second, it has proven to be a prophetic statement, for it was impossible for Vesalius to know—as we know—the impact of the future work that he alludes to, a text still five years away. Vesalius's statement does not suggest a full knowledge of what that "something greater" is, yet it indicates clearly that he sensed the momentum of a driving force within himself, a recognition of destiny's call.

The *Tabulae* was intended to present a visual teaching aid, but the unwritten message from Vesalius to his audience is nothing short of uncanny: *You, the audience, look closely at these images. Let yourself be drawn into them, as I am when I find them in the flesh. See how fascinating my world is and see how you, who have never seen, now know that which was unknowable in yourself. We are becoming something still unknown, but we are coming.*

Of the numerous copies printed in 1538, only two complete copies of the *Tabulae* are known to exist today. All others, it is suspected, were used and worn into nonexistence.

iii. Intellectual Rewrite

Just as Vesalius experienced frustration when copies of the *Tabulae* were reproduced in great volume without his permission, Vesalius himself would incur the anger of his former teacher, Guinter van Anderach, when he revisited and revised the 1536 translation of Galen's *Institutiones*, a text to which Vesalius had previously contributed.

In the two years following the original publication of Guinter's edition of *Institutiones*, Vesalius had been using the work in his anatomy lectures. It was during this close examination of the text, in combination with his work in dissection, that Vesalius realized that many of Galen's explanations were reflective of various animal, rather than human, anatomical structures. Vesalius's revelation was this: if theoretical knowledge is based on objective truths, then those truths should be verifiable through empirical study—autopsy and dissection being the best way to check speculation.

Vesalius introduced his 1538 publication of the *Tabulae* as a pedagogical tool that could be utilized in the instruction of anatomical theory. This was also the purpose of his unauthorized edition of Guinter's *Institutiones anatomicae*, released later that same year. In the two years following his work with Guinter on the first edition, Vesalius immersed himself in study, reading as many medical texts as possible and exploiting every opportunity to perform dissections. As a professor, Vesalius made a point of recommending Guinter's anatomical handbook to his students as a means of supplementing his lectures and dissection demonstrations, calling the text "exceedingly useful and necessary, since this [Galen's *Institutiones*] has been handed down and perfected by Galen in nearly forty books."[120] In speaking of Guinter's edition, Vesalius says this in the preface to his own edition:

> Inasmuch as I perceived that because of the difficulty
> and prolixity of the matter, very few peruse it sedulously,
> I began to consider what path might lead to this easily
> accessible field; none seemed better to me than that which
> Johannes [Guinter] had smoothed and laid out for this
> purpose.[121]

Vesalius speaks with admiration of his teacher, but as the reader may recall, Guinter was not highly regarded for his skills in dissection and was considered a better teacher than butcher. Vesalius had played an instrumental role in providing research for Guinter's first edition, and since Vesalius had been using the text in his classes, it is reasonable that he would want the text to reflect *his* improved knowledge of the field and to correct claims that he knew were not true. In gracious form, however, Vesalius explains in the preface to his second edition that the fault of the original text was not that of his former teacher and that his only reason for returning to the text was for the sake of his students.

> [E]ven [Guinter's] work, due to the excessive haste
> demanded by the printers and their negligence, is not
> free from errors; I therefore thought that I would be
> undertaking a work greatly desired by all students, if I
> should through my diligence cause the (fruit of the) vigils
> of this man of great merit in studies to appear (again)
> in corrected and authoritative form. Many begged me
> to do this. I trust to the liberality of the author who, I
> think, will not be offended by this, since I have received
> the major part of my studies from him—a teacher both
> most liberal and most learned. In what measure I have
> excelled here, I shall not say; I have desired to perform
> a service for the benefit of many—and those who will
> read this with (fair) judgment and candid spirit will, I
> think, agree with me (in that respect). Of my experience
> in dissection I shall say nothing, because there are many
> witnesses to testify to what I have done in this field, for

> I have conducted anatomical (courses) in the three most
> celebrated of European universities which I have visited
> for the purpose of (advanced) study.[122]

Before the revolution of the printing press, the concept of authorial ownership of the content of a text did not formally exist.[123] As a result, in the infancy of the publishing industry, abuses were frequent and for those exploited, as Vesalius knew, well noted by the original authors.[124] In the above quote, Vesalius clearly identifies the intellectual property of the text as belonging to Guinter, but this appears to be a gesture of good will, not a necessary procedure legitimizing the newer edition. Understood in this light, Vesalius's recognition of Guinter also serves to avoid, if not a legal conflict, then a professional one, first, by informing the audience of the original source of the material, and second, by appealing to Guinter's "liberality" in hopes that the new edition and its justifications are not received by his teacher as an affront.

Although there were legitimate issues around the typography of the original edition, Vesalius also took to expanding on many points that he felt had been insufficiently dealt with, particularly in relation to dissection techniques, while omitting others. With such a clear altering of the original text, it is understandable that Vesalius was concerned with how his efforts would appear to the original author.

It is not certain what Guinter's response was to Vesalius's revised edition of *Institutiones*; however, there is some evidence that it was not altogether positive. Though publicly gracious to Vesalius, Guinter took to revising the *Institutiones* yet again in 1539 (just one year following Vesalius's edition) and included some, but not all, of Vesalius's revisions. Additionally, when approached in 1539 to reedit Guinter's Latin translation of the *Opera Galeni—Anatomical Procedures*—for the Giunta Press, Vesalius was reluctant to accept. The project's supervising editor, Augustinus Gadaldinis, reported that Vesalius had to be strongly persuaded to take on the project because he was "obsessed" with the "fear of giving offence to his teacher Andernach."[125] This resistance seems to suggest that Guinter had, however indirectly, expressed some degree of displeasure with Vesalius's previous adaptation of his work.

Regardless of the relationship between Guinter and Vesalius, through his edition of the *Institutiones*, Vesalius once again makes it clear to his audience that he is an authority on the material presented. Without asking for permission or suggesting to Guinter that he publish a second edition, Vesalius took it upon himself to revise the original edition in order to correct previous errors and to apply the knowledge that he had derived from dissection to the erroneous assumptions of the first publication. Vesalius's most significant and controversial assertion within the new edition of Guinter's text was that Galen's anatomical theory was derivative of animal anatomy and stood in stark contrast to human anatomical structures. This was a radical deviation from conventional medical dogma and a highly contentious move for Vesalius. Unlike the *Tabulae*, Vesalius's edition of the *Institutiones* allowed him to present himself as both a scholar and an anatomist and marked Vesalius's coming into his own before the medical community.

Having altered so much of Guinter's original material, Vesalius felt compelled to correct another oversight of the first edition among the clarifications and expanded passages added to the second edition: the credit bestowed upon Vesalius by his teacher no longer appeared marginal as it had in the original text. Nietzsche once wrote, "a student repays his teacher badly by remaining a student"; Guinter, it seems, did not share this sentiment.

iv. Where to Cut?

When Vesalius returned to the Louvain in order to complete his bachelor's degree in medicine, having previously studied under the leading Galenic scholars of Paris, he found himself substantively caught up in the debate over the practice of venesection. What began as an open discussion between him and a junior member of Louvain's faculty, Jeremiah Drivère, quickly became a vocal and obstinate contest between the faculty's scholars and physicians, many of whom had published widely on the subject. It would not be until 1539 in his *Letter on Venesection* that Vesalius would publicly expound his position and detail the heated exchanges between him and his colleague.

In terms of professional milestones, Vesalius's first year as a professor at Padua marked a prolific time in the young professional's career and life. Between the fall of 1537 and the summer of 1538, Vesalius successfully passed his doctoral exams with distinction, performed the school's winter public anatomy seminar, assumed a professorial position at the university, conducted numerous lectures and private dissections, and brought to print two works of significant achievement—the illustrated *Tabulae* and the revised edition of Guinter's *Institutiones*. Yet despite these exhaustive accomplishments, the end of the 1538 academic term did not see Vesalius seeking respite from his work. Instead, Vesalius accepted the invitation of his mentor, Nicholas Florena, to formally contribute to the debate over bloodletting, a topic that had been the focus of much of his previous year's work.

Although the procedure sounds barbaric to contemporary ears, from antiquity until the late nineteenth century, venesection was the "sheet anchor of therapeutics"[126] in the treatment of the humoral system. Grounding their arguments in the wisdom of Greek writers, each side of the debate found evidence to support its conclusions. Effectively, the ideological battle lines were drawn between those who believed the traditional Arabic translations of Hippocratic and Galenic texts, which stated that the vein should be cut as far as possible from the site of infection, and those who advocated the newly rediscovered Greek texts and their Latin translations, which suggested that the vein closest to the infection should be cut. Based on his understanding of the venous system, Vesalius came to conclude with much conviction that the latter position was correct. But unlike most of his contemporaries in the debate, Vesalius's belief was not the product of long deliberation, personal bias, or intuition; instead it was the result of firsthand research and empirical study of the human body.

Vesalius, as a student and a teacher of Galen's work, maintained an ideological commitment to Galen that blinded much, but not all, of his efforts to see in the body what his ears could not hear. However, "no part of Galen's anatomy [was] more vulnerable and unsatisfactory than his description of the venous system."[127] Because venesection was so central to many therapeutic treatments of the time and because its method was subject to considerable debate, the venous system had for many years been the object of Vesalius's careful inquiry. As a result, it was not long before Galen's "infallible" account of the human vascular system began to seem unlikely. In the *Tabulae* and the *Institutiones*, Vesalius demonstrated the substance of his position on bloodletting, and in the process, established himself as the foremost expert on the debate.

Vesalius's engagement with the issue of bloodletting focused on how venesection techniques should be applied to the treatment of pleurisy or *dolor lateralis*.[128] Following the traditional authority of medieval practitioners—most notably Avicenna, a Persian physician born in 980 CE—many believed that pleurisy could be successfully treated if the patient was bled from a vein at the site most remote from the inflammation. Treatment by this logic often entailed making an incision in the foot or big toe on the side opposite the patient's chest pain. This technique remained relatively unchallenged until, in 1514, a Parisian physician, Rene Brissot, found success in treating an "epidemic" of pleurisy by following his own interpretation of Hippocrates' and Galen's instructions: Instead of slowly bleeding the patient, drop by drop, from a remote site, Brissot opened the vein in the arm nearest the infected side. Although his success sparked a significant local debate on venesection, it was not until the 1525 postmortem publication of his interpretation and associative method that the controversy spread across Europe. Since venesection was a cornerstone therapy of the accepted medical community, many leading physicians and scholars of the day felt compelled to take a position on the subject. Siding with Brissot were Johannes Manardus, Leonard Fuchs, and Matthaeus Curtius—the "Lutherans of physicians."[129].

While finishing his medical studies at the University of Louvain, Vesalius found himself immersed in the volatile and divisive debate over which venesection technique should be practiced. But it was not until after a purposeful visit with one of the "most celebrated men" of his age, Matthaeus Curtius, that Vesalius felt compelled to formally enter the ring of discussion.[130] An esteemed and renowned physician and professor at the University of Bologna, Curtius invited Vesalius, in 1538, to stay in Bologna from August to October and "refresh" himself after an intense scholastic year. As he had extensively dissected, studied, and published his firsthand accounts of the structure and function of the human venous system, the young scholar welcomed the opportunity to meet and discuss the pressing medical issues of the day with the highly revered scholar, particularly since both were in professional agreement with Brissot on the subject of venesection.

By Saunders and O'Malley's account, their meeting initially went very well. Curtius, who had addressed the problem of using venesection in treating internal inflammations such as pleurisy, showed Vesalius three published editions of his latest commentaries on the subject.[131] Although each was in general agreement with the other, a significant divide sprang up between the two men in relation to a matter of interpretation. What did Hippocrates mean (as he was represented in Galen's translations) when he instructed that the sectioning (cutting) of the vein should be made "in-line" or "according to the straightness"?[132] The consensus among Brissot's supporters—Curtius included—was that "straightness" implied making incisions in relation to particular alignments of the body, while Vesalius, who had intimate knowledge of the azygos vein which "fed" the affected areas in question, asserted that "straightness" referred to making incisions that would preserve the "straightness and continuity of the fibres" that constituted the vein.[133] The existence of these "fibres" played a significant role in the theory of clinical bloodletting and practice, and remained a major point of grievance between Vesalius and Curtius throughout much of their lives. Following his visit, Vesalius returned to Padua and did not see Curtius again until 1540, the year following the publication of the *Venesection Letter,* at a reunion that proved to be far less congenial than their first introduction.

Following Vesalius's return to Padua, Nicholas Florenas, doctor to Charles V and the Royal House of Naples, asked Vesalius to formally explain a reference he made in the margins of Tabula II of the *Tabulae* regarding the treatment of *dolor lateralis* through venesection. Reluctant to publish a text on the issue of bloodletting, Vesalius chose instead to formulate a response in such a way as to allow him to fully articulate his position, while simultaneously protecting himself from direct public scrutiny and debate: Vesalius wrote Florenas a letter, dated January 1, 1539. The letter was published four months later.

In the opening lines of his correspondence to Florenas, Vesalius expresses his reluctance to expose himself to the reactions of the public, who would most certainly oppose his findings. If his visit with Curtius in Bologna had convinced him of anything, it was that he could not trust even the humanists to side with him. Vesalius thus appears to his voyeuristic audience to be a reluctant participant, coerced into the debate. Vesalius was generally not afraid to challenge the conventions of the day; however, because his position on venesection was part of a broader challenge to the authority of the Galenic tradition, he likely desired to dodge the scrutiny of those who would oppose him until his research was complete and his defense, fully articulated.

Though masked as an informal correspondence, Vesalius's letter was a carefully crafted treatise on venesection, which he must have suspected would be published in the form of an *epistolae*.[134]

> As you well know, even the most erudite dispute fiercely among themselves, with unbridled enthusiasm and by contentious subtlety in open and wordy contradictions, on the place of venesection in *dolor lateralis*; and to such an extent that few physicians of any reputation are to be found who have not undertaken to publish some example of their cleverness in this affair, thereby engendering among their opponents the most atrocious charges and envious attack.[135]

Nevertheless, Vesalius says he will write:

> privately and more extensively my opinion on this matter (although cursorily and hurriedly). But I shall wait for some other time before committing myself and my practice to public debate. However, in other respects I consider the matter to be of a kind which needs neither lengthy handling nor diversified demonstration, for, apart from the principles of others, it depends mainly upon the very careful inspection of dissections.[136]

The sentiment presented above is twofold: At once Vesalius expresses a hesitance to enter the discourse on venesection which is dominated, he says, by ill-conceived theories and those who rightfully challenge them; yet at the same time, he is dismissive of the discussion at large, suggesting that the question of venesection is only for those who have not bothered to look directly to the body, as he has done. These opening comments seem to speak to a general reader who requires a broad contextualization of the issue, complete with formal niceties, and not a correspondence to a family friend in response to a question of clarification. That he so adamantly overstates his lack of interest in entering public debate seems to reflect the psychological symptom manifest in the adage, "thou dost protest too much."

The overly formal structure of the letter's presentation further supports this reading of the text. For example, following the publishing etiquette of the day, Vesalius begins by acknowledging the contributions of others in the field, while remaining modest as it relates to his own achievements, a gesture that parallels the prefaces of his publications. This is particularly evident in Vesalius's explicit praise of Matthaeus Curtius, who "sweated and laboured long and with untiring effort to recover and to recall from the most profound darkness into the light the true opinion of Hippocrates and Galen on Venesection."[137] Being mindful of Vesalius's recent falling-out with Curtius, a knowing reader must question whether this is a tongue-in-cheek shot directed at Curtius or whether Vesalius was in fact naive enough to believe that Curtius could possibly receive his words as anything but antagonistic. Regardless of Vesalius's intentions, Curtius's reception of the *Venesection Letter*—appearing in the form of a scathing review—was quite spiteful.

The body of Vesalius's essay begins pro forma with praise for the work of the fathers of medicine, Hippocrates and Galen. Providing ample citations from each writer throughout his treatise, Vesalius nonetheless deviates from them significantly by weaving into his discourse a meticulous description of the azygos vein, which he had observed during dissection. As this detail was pivotal to his interpretation of Hippocrates' bloodletting technique, Vesalius supplements his account with a detailed illustration of how the unpaired vein feeds the ribs in the human body. The insight that his research brought to the subject, and the strength that it gave to his conviction, prompted Vesalius to insist that firsthand empirical analysis of the human body should direct the interpretation of the Greek master's texts.

> [I]n the arrangement of the veins, it behooves each and every physician to observe these things from the anatomy of bodies and not like our Aesculpains [certain physicians], relying solely on a pile of authorities and without exact knowledge of the veins to be sectioned in disease, to fight and brawl with their adversaries like the Andabatae [gladiators]. I know, among others, a certain person who had the temerity to write against the opinion of Galen on venesection in *dolor lateralis* before he had seen an anatomy, even in a dream.[138]

Despite the fevered opposition to Vesalius's radical interpretation of Hippocrates' venesection technique, he maintains a simple defense: "[T] o this question of the origin of the vein I can add no other testimony except ocular belief."[139] By grounding his stinging criticisms and confident conclusions in empirical demonstrations, Vesalius effectively *reconstitutes* the venesection argument. That is, he relocates the venesection discourse in such a way that opposition to his theory must take the form of an independent and direct confrontation with the physical reality referenced. Since Vesalius's findings were the product of research through autopsy, only evidence derived from the process of dissection could undermine his conclusions.[140] He was not the only proponent of empirical research at the time, but Vesalius was unique in that he publicly mandated, through the illustration of a highly disputed therapeutic practice, the adoption of a new methodology of anatomical analysis for those presenting or contesting issues of medical "fact."

Early in the piece, Vesalius makes a point to characterize a particular class of academic who—without reflection—criticizes his work: "[W] hatever the subject may be [they attack] new and heterodox opinions."[141]

Vesalius is specifically addressing Drivière from Louvain, who was most vocal in his opposition to humanist thought and whose knowledge base was, as Vesalius characterized it, "in his own opinion very learned and extraordinarily self-satisfied, for what accomplishments I do not know."[142] Vesalius continues:

> [I]n a crowded assembly of the most erudite men [Drivière] was not ashamed to call Manardus, Fuchs, Curtius, and Brissot the Lutherans of physicians because I, relying on the authority of their public pronouncements, had attacked, perhaps too sharply, his conclusion on venesection. Although they, with the great energy and no little personal expense, have restored the ancient Hippocratic rationale of therapy from former ignorance and barbarism, the virtuous fellow believes that they should, as the Lutherans of medicine, be ridiculed with every sort of injustice and on every pretext. Indeed, inflated with self-assured knowledge and with exceptional arrogance, he was accustomed to despise everyone else and to offer I know not what heresies, being incapable of anything else. He used to proclaim unashamedly that he had to employ words from the common dung-heap to suit such barbarians lest we, not yet Candidates, be infected by this sort of pestiferous decay. But whatever he and similar crickets might chirp I care not a straw.[143]

Although it appears that Drivière's reference to "Lutherans of physicians" is meant to be derogatory, Vesalius redeems the accused—himself included—by rightfully equating Lutherans (church reformers) with humanists (academic reformers), whom he credits with restoring "the ancient Hippocratic rationale of therapy from former ignorance and barbarism." Both Vesalius and Drivière recognized the intimate relationship between the evolving religious and scholastic reforms of their day, but Drivière's ignorance and arrogance are epitomized in his undignified use of insults and language "from the common dung-heap." It may appear to the reader that Vesalius is reducing himself to the level of his adversary by returning to these distasteful events so long after the fact, but Vesalius includes these comments at the start of his address in order to demonstrate how violent and irrational Drivière, and others like him, have been in their attack on progressive intellectuals like himself. Additionally, it is undoubtedly an attempt to humiliate Drivière by presenting his audacity and repugnant behavior to the larger public sphere. In a time when the eloquence of argument and debate was revered, Drivière's comments fell dreadfully far below his standing.

As the letter draws to a close, Vesalius speaks of his current project and the limits set upon it:

> We have now also finished the two tables on the nerves; in the first, the seven pairs of cranial nerves have been [89] drawn and in the other all the small branches of the dorsal medulla, expressed. I consider that these must be kept until we undertake the tables on the muscles and on all the internal parts. We have tried in the present year a plan by which this can be done very conveniently, but in such a crowd of spectators that is was entirely impossible to complete the task. If there existed here the opportunity for bodies which once could be obtained elsewhere, the studious would no longer need to work without profit, since so many celebrated men encourage and invite me daily to understand the field.[144]

If we remain under the assumption that Vesalius anticipated the essay's publication, then his words read as a direct appeal, presumably to the medical faculty at Padua, to allow him greater access to bodies for dissection. By suggesting that his lack of opportunity to work with cadavers is the only obstacle standing between him and further success, and by adding that the university and city would benefit financially by assisting him (due to his popularity among the elite and influential), Vesalius cleverly argues for more resources to facilitate his continued studies. He implies that his achievements reflect on Padua and its university as much as they do his own efforts. And it seems Vesalius's message was indeed heard. Following the publication of his letter, and a coincidental change in Padua's civic leadership,[145] Vesalius found that he had an ample supply of cadavers to work with.

Contemporary scholars, Saunders and O'Malley, who have translated and studied the *Venesection Letter,* argue that it bears witness to Vesalius's transition from a Galenist who used dissection as a means of confirming Galen's theories, to a confident researcher whose observations, derived from repeated dissection, "enable[d] him to challenge with growing confidence the infallibility of the Prince of Physicians."[146] Additionally, they assert that, because Vesalius based his arguments on anatomical "facts" derived from sense observation, anyone thereafter wishing to "attack the Vesalian theory effectively . . . must adopt the new objective method of dissection."[147] Although Vesalius's observations were not always accurate, he in effect gave voice to a new empirical science of anatomy, which left even his own conclusions open to further validation. For example, in his discussion of his current studies, Vesalius makes reference to the issue of whether the heart and arteries contract simultaneously or synchronously. Insisting that his vivisection of living animals revealed that arteries contracted "at odds and contrary,"[148] he supports a conclusion very much in line with conventional beliefs at the time. This theory held until 1616 when William Harvey introduced his theory of the circulatory system—that blood circulated around the body through the pumping of the heart—a conclusion in direct contradiction to Galenic theory.[149] However wrong Vesalius may have been in the essence of this theory and others, the method that he purported as the necessary basis of all anatomical knowledge—observation through dissection—grew to become the foundation of all modern medical discoveries. By raising the import of methodology above the details of revealed conclusions, Vesalius would also find himself positioned as his own critic. In his advanced study of the venous system, Vesalius was forced to admit that his earlier assumption relating to the existence of fibers in the veins was in fact erroneous. In light of this discovery, Vesalius said of the controversy of venesection, in which he had invested greatly, that it amounted to "in large part goat's wool."[150]

Although the end of the sixteenth century would witness the beginning of the end of the practice of bloodletting, it was not completely abandoned as a therapeutic procedure until the end of the nineteenth century. The inability to definitively determine which venesection procedure was the "best" or "most correct" curative method led Spain, for example, to outlaw the new Brissot-inspired practice. It is difficult from today's vantage point to understand what was at stake in the venesection debate, but it is necessary to point out that the fervor that surrounded the discourse was in many respects representative of a larger conflict of the age: traditionalists were forced to defend themselves against those whose empirical groundings threatened to destroy, not simply their long-held practices and beliefs, but also their social standing, their legitimacy as scholars and physicians, and the world as they knew it. Vesalius would be an important agent of this change.

v. War of the Worlds

Following the publication of the *Venesection Letter*, the University of Padua formally recognized the cumulative contribution that Vesalius had brought to the field of medicine, both as a scholar and a teacher. For having "aroused such admiration in [his] students," Vesalius found his salary nearly doubled in October of 1539.[151] But his popularity was not limited to the students of Padua. In January of 1540, at the request of the medical students at the University of Bologna, Vesalius began a series of anatomical demonstrations intended to accompany Professor Curtius's lectures on Mundino's treaties. Thanks to the notes of Baldasar Heseler, a medical student in attendance, there remains today a detailed account of each of Vesalius's twenty-six demonstrations. In the summary preface to his notes, Heseler observed of Vesalius:

> Partly after Galen, partly through his own discoveries and research he corrected many false opinions very carefully by means of the dissection of three human bodies and six dogs and other animals, and showed the doctors and us students many things neither heard of nor seen before.[152]

As has been well documented, Vesalius was true to his duty and referenced Curtius's lecture material during his demonstrations, but he rid himself of the responsibility quickly by covering most of the material over the first few expositions. Vesalius's main interest and intention at the time was directed to the dissection of the muscles and internal organs. While Curtius pontificated for hours on the internal structures of the body—liberally citing and comparing multiple classical authorities as a means of explaining the superiority of Galen through Mondino—Vesalius addressed the same material only marginally, preferring to focus his time on the dissections at hand.

Vesalius began each demonstration by lecturing "at great length and exhaustively" on the nature of what he was about to demonstrate. An articulated skeleton hanging close at hand allowed Vesalius to clearly address the relationship of the individual muscles to the underlying bone structures "so that we should afterwards better understand the beginning and end of the muscles."[153] He also utilized the illustrations from the *Tabulae*, along with other sketches, to offer supplemental details during the presentations. Regarding the eighth demonstration, Heseler suggests that Vesalius's concentration on the muscles was to the exclusion of all other areas of interest: "Certainly, he was attentive only to the anatomy of the muscles, for everything else he passed as already known."[154] Vesalius's research at the time was focused primarily on documenting the structure of the human body's muscles and organs, so it is not surprising that he took advantage of the opportunity of this dissection series to advance his studies further. As he had already published the *Tabulae*, which clearly illustrated the venous structure and its associated networks, Vesalius may have felt that his time would be better served outlining new material. Still, the tension and competition that remained between Curtius and Vesalius inevitably returned the subject of venesection to the center of discussion.

On the occasion of one infamous lecture, Curtius systematically worked to undermine Vesalius's credibility by referring to him as a mere *anatomista* and liberally attacking his theories on venesection. When Curtius had finished with his lecture, Vesalius, who had been in the audience, rose from his seat and asked the *Domine* (Curtius) to accompany him to the anatomy theater so that he could demonstrate the truth of his theories.[155] As the following dialogue[156] outlines, the dissection and lecture on this particular day would not soon be forgotten.

"Now, *excellentissime Domine*," Vesalius began, "here we have our bodies. We shall see whether I have made an error. Now we want to look at this and we should in the meantime leave Galen, for I acknowledge that I have said, if it is permissible to say so, that here Galen is in the wrong, because he did not know the position of the vein without pair in the human body, which is the same today just as it was in his time."

To this, Curtius said, smiling, "No, *Domine*, we must not leave Galen because he always well understood everything, and consequently, we also follow him. Do you know how to interpret Hippocrates better than Galen did?"

"I do not say so, but I show you here in these bodies the vein without pair, how it nourishes all the lower ribs, except the two upper ones, in which there is no pleurisy." Vesalius knocked both hands against the middle of the chest, "For always here occurs inflammation and pleurisy, not at the two upper ribs." Vesalius continued, demonstrating the relationship of the vein to the heart and ribs and supporting his theory as to why the vein should be sectioned where he stipulated.

"I am no *anatomista*," Curtius mocked, "but there can be also other veins nourishing the ribs and muscles besides these."

"Where, please? Show them to me!"

"Do you want to deny the ducts of Nature?"

"Oh! You want to talk about things not visible and concealed. I again talk about what is visible."

"Indeed, I always deal with what is most obvious," said Curtius. "*Domine*, you do not well understand Hippocrates and Galen concerning this."

"It is quite true, because I am not so old a man as you are."

And so, according to Heseler, the two men accomplished nothing as their quarreling and scoffing continued.

At last Vesalius said, "*Domine* Doctor, I beg Your Excellency not to think me so unskilled that I do not know and understand this."

Smiling condescendingly, Curtius responded, "*Domine*, I did not say so, for I have said that you are excellent, but I have rejected the wrong explanation of Hippocrates implying that Galen should have erred in this."

"I acknowledge that I have said that Galen has erred in this, and this is evident here in these bodies, as also many other mistakes of his." Vesalius proceeded to demonstrate on the body more of its structures, while noting to his audience that anyone wishing to object to his theory should first understand it.

At the end of this highly spirited debate, each man is said to have made a gesture of civility before leaving the other to his work. In summarizing Vesalius's debate with Curtius and the opposition that he would continue to face throughout his life, it is best to recall the words of the father of morbid anatomy, Giovanni Morgagni: "Those who have dissected many bodies have at least learned to doubt; when others, who are ignorant of anatomy and do not take the trouble to attend to it are in no doubt at all."

Whether either teacher won the hearts and minds of those observing the exchange that day is, naturally, unknown; however, it is clear that Vesalius fought to ground the discussion in the artifact of the body rather than leaving it wrapped and veiled in the rhetoric of its speculative inheritance.

For those students wishing to further explore the art of dissection in areas perhaps dismissed in the formal demonstrations, Vesalius made himself available for informal discussions and anatomical displays. In one instance, the students supplied their instructor with a body for dissection, a French priest who had been liberated from his burial vault.[157] The students' commitment and enthusiasm helped contribute to Vesalius's work, for at their professor's subtle prompting, the students "broke into tombs and collected the unclaimed bodies from the mortuary in order to obtain bones for study."[158] Because of the variety of bones supplied by the students, Vesalius was able to observe, for example, that the "bones of the aged differ from those of youth, and those of youth from those of children."[159]

During his stay at Bologna, Vesalius resided with a friend and professor of medicine, Andreas Bianchi, whose hospitality he rewarded with a fully articulated ape skeleton, in addition to the articulated skeleton of the

French cleric. This dual presentation of skeletons was possibly the first tool by which concrete comparative anatomy could be undertaken,[160] and it necessarily "provided Vesalius with proof that Galen's description of the processes of the lumbar vertebrae was derived not from human but from animal sources."[161]

vi. Galen for Giunta

The year 1539 proved to be an important one for Vesalius, and his publication success did not go unnoticed. As mentioned above, Vesalius was solicited in that year by Agostino Gadaldino, the editor-in-chief of the famous Giunta Press, to update and edit a Latin translation of three critical works by Galen: *De nervorum* (*The Nerves*), *De venarum arteriarumque* (*The Arteries and Veins*), and most notably, *De anotomicis administrationibus* (*Anatomical Procedures*). Although one might assume that the prospect of editing a series of texts would not appeal to Vesalius, particularly when its timing promised to overlap with his own research schedule, Vesalius took up the project with enthusiasm, seeing it as both an honor and an asset to his current project work. Ironically, history would soon locate Vesalius's participation in this project as a turning point in the history of anatomy—the start of a post-Galenic era.

In competition with the esteemed Aldine Press of Aldus Manutius, printers of the first Greek edition of Galen's complete works in 1525, the Giunta Press was equally prestigious and the recognized leader of sixteenth-century Venetian printing and publishing.[162] As Latin, not Greek, was the privileged language for most physicians and scholars at the time, the Giunta family focused its efforts on developing and publishing a quintessential Latin edition of Galen's works. In order to fulfill this commitment, the Giunta Press sought to update its original edition to ensure that their text remained relevant in light of the newly recovered Greek Galenic manuscripts. Their first edition of Galen's work had been published in 1522, with the second edition appearing in 1528; however, it would be another thirteen years before the third edition, which included Vesalius's revisions, was introduced. The press intended that its 1541 edition of

Galen's works would be a significant improvement on all previous existing editions, and as such, would dictate the nature of all future discourse on Galen's theories.

It was Gadaldino who identified Vesalius and brought him to the Giunta family's attention. Despite his youth—Vesalius was only twenty-five—he had become the most "celebrated and distinguished contemporary professor of dissection" and was an obvious candidate to contribute to the newly proposed edition.[163] Not only had his previous publications, grounded as they were in Galen's work, demonstrated Vesalius's capacity for comprehensive scholarship and artistic rendering, but his credentials as a young professor of surgery and anatomy at Padua would endow the new addition with unprecedented distinction.

Vesalius would not be the only scholar to work on the edition: John Caius, a previous student of Padua and Vesalius's housemate at the time, was also employed to do research for the new edition. Although each was responsible for separate aspects of the text, together the two men waded diligently through volumes of Latin and Greek manuscripts in order to identify and clarify inaccuracies of Galen's anatomy found in previous Latin editions. The Giunta Press supplied its editors with some textual materials, but they found most of these to be of little use. In 1570, some thirty years later, Caius would reflect on how he and Vesalius had struggled to find relevant texts that could be used in their editing.

> These notes [from Giunta], although of little value to Vesalius and me, since they were basically unsound, nevertheless spurred us on to seek out other manuscripts. Upon searching, I discovered another Greek manuscript among Bessario's books in the library of San Marco in Venice. It was helpful in several places.[164]

Vesalius's formal goal—the objective presented by his publisher—was to present a Latin translation that was void of error and reflective of the most recent translations of Galenic texts. This process entailed clarifying the meaning and style of Galen's work and amending previous editions of the Latin translation by removing non-Galenic material, correcting corrupt interpretations, and incorporating newly translated material. Despite his having publicly identified errors in some of Galen's work, most notably in Guinter's *Institutiones*, Vesalius remained a student of Galenic anatomy.

Through this intense period of textual analysis, in combination with his own research in dissection, Vesalius repeatedly found himself confronted with contradictions between what he *believed* to be true and what he *saw* before him. In a letter, Gadaldino insists that despite Vesalius's previous hesitation to alter too much of Guinter's translation for fear of offending him (yet again), Vesalius nonetheless succumbed to necessity and effectively "remade" the edition.[165] Unlike Vesalius, visionary that he was, Caius remained very much a student of his time. As an adamant loyalist to Galenic authority, Caius felt Vesalius's undermining of Galen was nothing short of blasphemy. Believing that Galen's insight was fundamentally infallible, Caius responded to Vesalius with the mantra of the loyalists, insisting that if errors did exist in the work, they were the product of previous editors who had inadvertently corrupted the texts and created a legacy of mistranslated material. Caius later described how he was formally at odds with some of Vesalius's editorial decisions, asserting that in certain parts of the text, Vesalius himself "corrupted" Galen's text and its meaning. However, subsequent editors of the *Opera Galeni* did not challenge Vesalius's work and left his contributions effectively untouched.

The controversy over whether or not Vesalius altered the integrity of the original Galen texts remains in the realm of speculation, but it is likely that he incorporated small corrections into *De nervorum* and *De venarum arteriarumque* as these were his particular areas of specialty. It does appear that, while working on the third section (*De anotomicis administrationibus*) however, Vesalius's primary focus was not to alter, but to clarify, the meaning and style of Galen's text, and, using the available Greek sources, amend the Latin text, delete non-Galenic material, revise corrupt phrases, and add material that he judged authentic. As was appropriate for developing a new edition of another's work, particularly a highly revered classical authority, Vesalius did not explicitly point out in his revisions any instances where his own research led him to conclude that Galen had erred. Such comments he rightly saved for his own work.

The opposition to his work and the blind commitment to Galenic authority that Vesalius experienced while working and living with Caius is characteristic of many of his interactions within academic circles. Unable or unwilling to accept what Vesalius objectively was able to demonstrate, both through dissection and detailed illustration, many students, colleagues, and even friends—as was the case with Caius—would decidedly separate themselves from Vesalius. After eight months of working and living together, Vesalius and Caius parted ways.

Chapter Six

The Fabrica

As has been detailed above, Vesalius's life was in many respects shaped by his being born into a family of royal medical professionals during a time of humanist scholarship, a social phenomena that was given wings through the advent of print. Yet Vesalius was clearly unique in his ambitions, his dedication to scholarship, and his mission to advocate for knowledge that was grounded in verifiable empirical evidence. What made Vesalius so special was his compulsion to move forward in his pursuit of anatomical knowledge, a goal that developed through an opening within himself. In an age and culture where so much of one's life was already articulated for the individual—including his or her mode of dissidence, as categorized through broad labels within the religious and academic reformation—Vesalius was able to create, in the midst of all the structures and mandates around him, a clearing where the pervasive ideological noise of the world was muted, and the human body, as it was, could appear. The *Fabrica* was Vesalius's map to this serene clearing.

By 1540, well versed in classical and Galenic theory, Vesalius's analysis of the raw material of the human body established in his mind's eye the form and substance of a project that would be the culmination of all of his work to date. By remaining intellectually immersed in the very fissure that threatened to crack open the world of medicine and anatomical theory, Vesalius created a space for himself in history.

The task of creating a text unlike anything previously seen before—both in substance and in form—could only have been the product of an unrelenting drive and clear vision. The end product is remarkable enough, but following the project's path from its inception to its completion proves nothing short of astounding. Consequently it is useful to look to the creation of *De humani corporis fabrica* (*The Structure of the Human Body*) in terms of its constituting processes: research and analysis (textual and empirical); artistic representation; and printing and distribution. Naturally, these categories do not represent a linear unfolding of events, and each category does not exclude extensive consideration of the others; however, for the purpose of highlighting the achievements of the *Fabrica*, this structural breakdown will allow for a more comprehensive discussion of its production.

i. The Research

Following the completion of his editing responsibilities for the Giunta Press, Vesalius directed his own research to continued Galenic studies and theoretical considerations. In 1539 he was single-mindedly focused on furthering his understanding of Galen and other ancient and contemporary scholars in order to develop within himself a solid foundation in medical theory. But in 1541, Vesalius determined to step out into the open and systematically articulate the errors that he had come to believe were inherent to Galen's original anatomical theories. The previous three to four years of editing Galen had proven invaluable in guiding his own critical research in dissection. The sanctified texts of the classical scholars grounded the ideological strongbox that determined the common medical assumptions and practices of the day, but Vesalius's simultaneous work on and in the body allowed him to seek out direct confirmation of anatomical features as he went. When cadavers were not available, Vesalius focused on absorbing the theoretical material in question so as to more effectively utilize the decaying material when next he had opportunity to observe.

Though Vesalius had a significant volume of textual resources to draw from, some essential materials remained difficult to access. While employed by the Giunta Press, Vesalius generally received access to most of the texts that he wished to study; however, while working independently following the completion of his contract, he was occasionally denied such liberties. For example, Vesalius sought to consult a particular Greek text in order to clear up several ambiguous points presented in Galen's *On the Bones*, but the gatekeeper of the text refused to allow him access. Vesalius became so indignant over the incident that he formally castigated the men who had refused him the loan:

> Certain individuals unconcerned about the benefit of mankind or even jealous . . . conceal the Greek original so that under no circumstances, or at any time, would they allow me to consult it. Balamio and Cardinal Rodolfo admitted their possession [of the Greek text] but said it was in such condition that it could not be lent to me. However, I shall strive to get along without this book, as well as certain other works of Galen they have concealed to prevent their use, or more correctly—since they themselves can't use them—to provide food for worms.[166]

Despite his bitterness, it is unlikely that not having access to the manuscript impacted the final draft of the *Fabrica*, since Vesalius's account of the structure of the human skeleton (assuming bones were indeed the issue) represented some of his most accurate work, even without the privilege of the forbidden text.

The greatest obstacle to Vesalius's research was not inaccessible texts but the limited supply of human cadavers to examine. Vesalius often asserted the importance of dissecting animals for comparative purposes, but by no means did he believe animals were a substitute for human study. Having faulted Galen for relying solely on animal dissection, Vesalius too was forced to resort to them when human cadavers were not available. In preparing for the *Fabrica*, Vesalius found himself faced with the dilemma that he and Galen shared: in the absence of knowledge based on human dissection, should one substitute animal anatomy?

When access to cadavers was not an issue, the body's rate of decomposition was. Thus the process of dissection became an economical one, forcing Vesalius to prioritize his research goals as he went—the consequence of studying an organic object that remained useful only within certain parameters of putrefaction. This inescapable inconvenience likely explains why in the first two books of the *Fabrica*, the illustrations and explanations of the skeletal framework and the outline of the muscles are much more elaborate than those of the inner organs, systems, and tissues, which would have been more advanced in their decomposition by the time Vesalius reached them in the dissection process. On the other hand, Vesalius may have felt that some areas of the body required less attention. As we recall from his guest dissection series at Bologna, Vesalius labored over the structures of the muscles for so long that other areas of the body's interior were addressed only in a cursory manner, if at all.

It is believed that, in the production of the *Fabrica*, Vesalius felt rushed for time, but it is not certain whether his schedule was dependent on personal or professional deadlines. Having negotiated a one-year sabbatical from Padua in order to prepare his book for publication, it is possible that he was under extreme pressure to return to the university in time for the following school year. This would not be an easy goal to achieve, since Vesalius would have to travel to Venice in order to see his manuscript printed.

Most discussions on Vesalius concentrate on his academic adoption of dissection; however, he was above all a scientist and thus was fundamentally an observer of all kinds of natural phenomena. For example, Vesalius closely followed the development of representation in artist communities and was interested in how artists depicted the structures and forms of the body, particularly superficial musculature. While in Bologna, Heseler recorded that Vesalius preferred the representations of the ancients to those of contemporary artists. In demonstrating the muscles of the back, Vesalius noted that:

> large muscles of the back, the upper arm, the shoulder, etc, which our native artists of to-day do not represent so beautifully, can best be seen in the ancient monuments and antiquities of the ancient artists.[167]

Vesalius also remained attentive to the details of his daily life and the states of his own body. In the preface to the *Fabrica*, he gives brief attention to the painful emergence of his wisdom teeth. "As I write my thirty-second tooth is erupting in my twenty-sixth year."[168] He then confirms for his reader that his dilemma is commonplace for many adults, a conclusion he was able to determine through his study of the numerous skulls that he had procured from various cemeteries. He also advised his students to study their own bodies by palpating themselves in order to observe the physiological response; to concentrate on how the ribs and connective cartilages moved during breathing; and to compress various nerves in their arms and hands so as to produce numbness in particular areas. Closely observing the bodies of others was also of great benefit in creating awareness of anatomical anomalies. For example, Vesalius questioned why some men were able to wiggle their ears and others not. Why did some have double-jointed fingers? And why did some have the square-shaped heads of beggars? For Vesalius, any opportunity, even observing the cut of beef served at dinner, could contribute to the development of insight into the human anatomy.

His personal mandate to determine truths through successive empirical studies was evident as he discussed why he would not dare correct Galen's observations until he had studied and lectured on the specific subject at least three times: "I am not accustomed to say anything with certainty after only one or two observations."[169] Although it is unlikely that the audience of the *Fabrica* would have opportunity to observe what they were studying even once—much less three times—they were fortunate to have Vesalius's extensive observations available to them. But would they—could they—believe what they were seeing?

ii. Anatomy of a Masterwork

Between 1540 and 1541, Vesalius determined a working outline for the *Fabrica*. His overarching goal was to create a comprehensive, fully illustrated anatomy text that would build on Galen's anatomical foundation. Every aspect of Galen's extensive anatomical descriptions was to be examined in the light of evidence obtained through hands-on dissections. In setting this objective, Vesalius aimed to empirically confirm and expand on Galen's theories, if true, and to correct and clarify his theories when objective evidence suggested they were not accurate. What Galen had not seen, Vesalius would introduce in hopes of furthering medical and anatomical knowledge. Just as navigators were exploring and mapping the earth, Vesalius was exploring and "mapping" the human body. Both were seen as artifacts of God's creation, but the human body, created in God's image, the temple of the soul, stood as the apex of the Creator's wonders. It was Vesalius's desire to translate his years of laborious analysis into an anatomical atlas that could demonstrate both visually and textually the divine wonders of the human body.

Prior to the *Fabrica*, most anatomical texts followed the order adopted by Mondino for dissection and began with the viscera (the structures that decayed most quickly), proceeding outward, and then ending with the extremities and bones. Rather than devising an original order of presentation, or following the most conventional one, Vesalius structured his book in the manner of his own dissection presentations: in the order that Galen had adopted himself. This approach addressed the body from the inside out, beginning with the bones of the human skeleton, progressing to the muscles, then the arterial and venous system, the nervous system, the "organs of nutrition and generation, the heart and lungs, and finally the brain and the organs of sense." Throughout the *Fabrica*, Vesalius provides exhaustive information about the parts of the body but also gives exact directions for the process of dissection, allowing others to confirm his findings for themselves should they desire to. His hundreds of detailed accounts of the various stages of autopsy identify the various anatomical parts as they are revealed. Through this detailed method of instruction, Vesalius articulates the entire process of his work and lays bare before his audience the source and support of his authority.

The final outline of the *Fabrica* appeared in print as follows:

> In the first book I have described the nature of all the
> bones and cartilages, which because the other parts are
> supported and stabilized by them and are described
> in accordance with them, are the first to be learned

by students of Anatomy. The second book records the
ligaments by which bones and cartilages are connected to
each other, and then the muscles, producers of voluntary
motion. The third includes the highly complex series of
veins which carry familiar blood to the muscles, bones,
and other parts for their nourishment, and of the arteries
that regulate the mixture of innate heat and vital spirit.
The fourth explains not only the distribution of nerves that
go to the muscles, but the branches of the others as well.
The fifth tells about the construction of the organs that
assist nutrition, which is accomplished by food and drink.
In addition, because of their proximity, it also contains the
instruments fashioned by the supreme Maker of things for
the succession of the species. The sixth is devoted to the
heart, fomenter of the vital faculty, and to the parts that
assist it. The seventh examines the harmony of the brain
and the organs of sense in such a way that the series of
nerves taking their origin from the brain, explained in the
fourth book, is not repeated.[170]

Vesalius outlines his pedagogical intentions by stating that he outlines
the "fullest knowledge of the parts of the human body in these seven
books, just as I should normally discuss it before a group of learned men
in this city [Padua] or Bologna."[171] The completed manuscript contained
nearly seven hundred pages and over two hundred illustrations.

The *Fabrica* was written in Latin, the preferred language of sixteenth-
century academic texts. Although Latin was inaccessible to most outside of
the clergy and academic circles, it was Vesalius's writing style that drove his
audience to feelings of alienation and frustration. As a scholar constituted
by and for humanist thought, Vesalius strove to achieve an elegant and
polished writing form like those of the classical stylists, such as the famous
Roman humanist and philosopher, Cicero (106-73 BCE). As a result,
Vesalius adopted flowery language and convoluted sentence structures that
continue to exhaust some readers and agitate others.

The *Fabrica* would become a publishing success, but its infamy was based more on the explanatory success of the illustrations than on the elaborate descriptions intended to lead the discussion. In addressing the text, Harvey Cushing, a twentieth-century scholar, instrumental in resurrecting Vesalius's contribution to science and medicine for contemporary audiences, suggests that, "As a book, the *Fabrica* has probably been more admired, and less read than any publication of equal significance in the history of science."[172] Perhaps it is for this reason that, until recently, little effort had been made to publish an English edition of the *Fabrica*.

At the moment, two projects are underway to remedy this absence: Two Australian scholars, Richardson and Burd, are currently working on a series of publications on the books of the *Fabrica*. Daniel Garrison and Malcolm Hast of Northwestern University are posting translations of the original 1543 edition of the *Fabrica* and its revised 1555 edition on their Web site. In reference to the complexity of Vesalius's writing style, Garrison reminds us that the *Fabrica* was a polemical book and as such inherited a polemical style that was "part of the Galenic tradition." Since much of the text was intended to uproot erroneously held beliefs based in the preeminent authority of Galenic theory, the discourse necessitated the style Vesalius adopted. Garrison supports this conclusion by pointing out that Vesalius reserves his "most elaborate and difficult Latin" for passages where he "goes on the attack."[173] Since the primary goal of the *Fabrica* was for Vesalius to articulate where Galen ended and he began, it is not surprising that his commitment to this end resulted in an excessive literary gesture on par with the extraordinary event of its exposition.

iii. *The Drawings of a Madman*

The goal of the *Fabrica* was to articulate clearly, both in words and images, the reality of the human body.

> I have made every effort for a single purpose: to be of use
> to as many people as possible in an extremely abstruse and
> no less arduous enterprise, and to provide as truthful and

complete an account as possible of the fabric of the human body, which is made not of ten or twelve different parts (as it seems to the casual observer), but of some thousand.[174]

As an integral part of presenting this "account," Vesalius included "illustrations of all the parts, inserted in the text of the discourse in such a way that they place the dissected body before the eyes of the students of nature's works."[175] The primary purpose of the illustrations was to provide a reference guide that would act as an extension of his anatomy instruction, allowing him to "expound anatomy to others with less difficulty."[176] Coordinated closely with the text, the illustrations were to "explain in sufficient detail the number, location, shape, size, makeup, connection to other parts, use, function, and many such features of each part of the human body whose nature we are accustomed to investigate as we dissect."[177] This was a daunting undertaking—and not only for Vesalius, who had envisioned it. For the artists and wood engravers who were called upon to produce such a huge volume of material, it was madness.

It is not known for certain which artist or artists were responsible for the now famous anatomical drawings of the *Fabrica,* and the question of their identify has vexed many a Vesalian and *Fabrica* scholar. Nowhere in the hundreds of pages of text does Vesalius identify the artist(s) or engraver(s) to whom he was so deeply indebted. In later years, Vesalius would say only that he had to "put up with the bad temper of artists and sculptors who made [him] more miserable than did the bodies [he] was dissecting."[178]

It is thought by many that Jan Stephan van Calcar, the same artist who collaborated with Vesalius on the *Tabulae,* is responsible for the large plates of the *Fabrica.* This suggestion is based on Vesalius's comment at the end of the *Venesection Letter* of 1539 in which he indicates that he would like to undertake a larger work—presumably the *Fabrica*—if Jan Stephan would be available to assist. The most convincing evidence that Stephan was the artist comes from it being recorded that Jan Stephan supplied the printing deposit for the *Fabrica,* although it is not known why. Yet some scholars dismiss even the possibility that he was the artist, insisting that the quality of the title page and full-size plates reflect a far more sophisticated artistry than was demonstrated in the illustrations of the *Tabulae*. As Jan Stephan was a mature artist of thirty-nine when he drew the skeletons of the *Tabulae*, critics believe it to be unlikely that he would have been able to improve his skills to such a sizable degree in the two years between works.

Despite the uncertainty as to who they were, it is generally believed that the artists who created the drawings for the *Fabrica* emerged from Titian's workshop, the school of the great Venetian master. Not only do various early sources associate the anatomical drawings of the *Fabrica* with Titian's workshop, but the style of the illustrations is consistent with the school's instruction. Whether or not Vesalius utilized the artists of one workshop or many, one thing is certain, he called upon the most talented artists of Venice to bring his vision into life. Make no mistake—the *Fabrica* was intended to be a masterpiece.

Although contemporary readers may find offense in Vesalius's failure to credit the creators of the *Fabrica*'s illustrations and woodcarvings, this was not an uncommon practice at the time. For the artisans of the sixteenth century, their art was their craft and as such, their work. Just as carpenters, gilders, goldsmiths, potters, and printers were commissioned to perform their particular skills anonymously for clients, so too were painters and draftsmen.[179] It is difficult to imagine today, but many of what are considered the greatest achievements of genius artisans, such as Michelangelo's Sistine Chapel paintings, were commissioned and contracted works with varying degrees of creative input from the artist. In fact, part of the epic story of the Sistine Chapel ceiling frescos centers around the conflict between the pope's expectations of the work he had commissioned and Michelangelo's assertion of his creative vision.[180] Although such conflicts characteristically engender the mythologies within which genius is located, most artists of Vesalius's time were craftsmen who were making a living as anonymous hirelings. In other words, for every Michelangelo or Titian who fought for the internal integrity of their work, scores of able draftsmen worked diligently to meet their client's demands. If it turned out that Stephan van Calcar was not available at the time of the *Fabrica*'s production, there undoubtedly remained a reasonable supply of available and competent artists for Vesalius to draw from.

Although finding artists could be a challenge, working with artists, as Vesalius implies above, was even more difficult, personality conflicts aside. Vesalius's primary demand of his artist(s) would have been to provide accurate and detailed representations. However, if the illustrations were to be accurate, the subjects of the work had to be seen directly. Scheduling the artists to work closely with him during numerous dissections, Vesalius diligently oversaw every detail of the illustrations' construction. A reasonably good draftsman himself, Vesalius may have also been able to guide each artist's creations based on his own visual accounts of the anatomical structures that he recorded in the artist's absence.

The guiding images of the *Fabrica* were intended to function both as mnemonic aids and as explanatory tools. Yet it must be said that, taken as a whole, the quality of the illustrations was inconsistent, presenting both phenomenal and marginal artistic efforts. Generally speaking, the first half of the *Fabrica* is where Vesalius's most impressive, extensive, and accurate arguments against Galen are articulated. Here we find clear evidence that Vesalius's research was based in the careful dissection of human subjects, and the illustrations reflect the value and intensity of the arguments being presented. This is not the case in the second half of the book, where Vesalius relies more heavily on animal anatomy and offers fewer amendments to Galen's work. Through comparative analysis, Vesalius concluded that Galen had not dissected human cadavers and had made only superficial observations of desiccated and injured human bodies. For the most part, Galen had relied on animal anatomy, leading inevitably to errors of interpretation and extrapolation.

Perhaps due to the rush to complete the *Fabrica* or the lack of available human cadavers, Vesalius remained very much aligned with Galen in the second half of the book, offering comparative drawings that juxtaposed animal and human bones. Vesalius's intention of demonstrating both the differences, and at times, radical similarities, between animal and human bones has been interpreted as a means by which he could inform his audience, with minimal antagonism, that the similarities between the anatomy of animals and humans reasonably explained Galen's (incorrect) assumption that animal and human anatomy were mutually applicable.

In this way, Vesalius appears conscientious and humble in his critique of Galen. Modern critiques of the text, however, free from concerns of etiquette, note that Vesalius falls victim to the very thing that he purports to remedy: Although he does make some reference to his own use of animal anatomy, there are instances in the text where he, like Galen, fails to note that he has supplemented his human anatomical discussion with findings derived from animal anatomy. This oversight is not surprising given the vast amount of anatomical research required for a book of this magnitude, but it does lead the reader to ask how and why it appears unreferenced as it does.

iv. Skeletons and Muscle Men

His extensive use of articulated skeletons makes it clear that Vesalius believed a comprehensive understanding of the body's skeletal structure was a necessary prerequisite to understanding the fabric of the body as a whole. The skeleton holds unique significance for the anatomist, for bones constitute the final and lasting artifacts of human life, which, after death, can become objects of extensive and unmediated examination. Unlike previously published skeletal depictions, including those found in his own work, the *Tabulae*, Vesalius depicts the skeletons in Book I of the *Fabrica* with an advanced attention to detail and with an artistic and symbolic sophistication that paradoxically situates the audience as both observer and subject: The viewer looks upon the image with admiration for the wonder of the representation, and then is confronted with the subjective awareness of one's own "impossible" death. One of these illustrations includes a detailed frontal view of an articulated skeleton, poised with a grave digger's shovel under his right arm. Another skeleton is shown from the side, resting his head on his left hand in contemplation of a skull sitting atop a grave; inscribed on the tomb is the following: "Genius lives on, all else is mortal." Finally, the last plate depicts the skeleton from behind, weeping in despair, presumably over the agony of his own mortality.

The most famous and visually provocative figures of the *Fabrica*'s Book II are undoubtedly those of the "muscle men." Through a sequence of figures with muscles splayed (called *échorchés*), Vesalius demonstrates the layered structure of the human body. Although similar drawings had been created and adopted by painters and sculptors for referential use, the structured succession of this type of illustration in the *Fabrica* was previously unknown to medical illustration, thus creating a new pedagogical mode of anatomical education. These illustrations presented to the audience an explanatory depiction of the nature of different muscle groups and their relationships to the body's skeletal structure without need of textual expositions. Like subjects of the skeletal plates, the muscle men possess both utility and an aesthetic appeal. Upon publication of the *Fabrica*, fascination with these drawings created an immediate demand for plagiarized fugitive copies.

The first illustration of the muscle men shows a male figure with the skin removed, revealing the muscle formation beneath; the second shows the *échorché* male body in profile with the arms extended so as to display different muscles and their insertion points. In this print, Vesalius uses letters to identify specific anatomical features referenced within the text; the third, fourth, fifth, and sixth plates depict the systematic detachment of various muscles from their anchors, peeled back to reveal the underlying structures of the different muscle groups.

Among the most infamous of the muscle men series is the seventh plate, where, in addition to showing the muscle groups, Vesalius also demonstrates how he suspended and prepared his cadavers for dissection.

> When I am about to undertake the dissection of a man I pass a strong cord under the lower jaw through each jugal bone to the vertex of the head, tied like a noose, and either more toward the forehead or the occiput, depending upon my desire to suspend the cadaver either with the head erect or depressed. I place the longer end of the noose across a pulley fixed to a beam of the room, and by it I draw the suspended corpse now higher now lower and take care that it may be turned in every direction in accordance with the requirements of the task; and again, when desired, I am able to rest it on a table, for the table

can easily be accommodated to the position of the pulley. It was in this way that the cadaver was suspended for the delineation of all the illustrations of muscles, just as the seventh illustration displays, although when that was delineated the rope was twisted back to the occiput for the sake of the muscles conspicuous there in the neck.[181]

In this illustration, a rope has also been added to display the scapula (shoulder blade) muscles and keep each from drooping like a "broken wing." In the final plate of the series, the figure is shown leaning back against the wall behind it. The figure, weakened from having been stripped of so many layers of flesh and muscle, now struggles to remain upright. Gone are the lush backgrounds and animated gestures of the previous plates; this final illustration offers only the image of a devastated body against a bleak and lifeless backdrop. Having displayed the muscles from the front and anterior of the body, the next four figures present a similar succession of images presenting the muscles as they are stripped away, but this time, as they appear from the back. The last image of this series depicts a final destitute figure, facing away from the viewer, kneeling upon a desolate platform by a skull and the partial remains of its once fully constituted body.

v. Death Never Looked So Good

For nearly six centuries, the illustrations of the *Fabrica* have provoked, engaged, and stunned its audiences. It is, of course, not simply the subject represented or the figures themselves that captivate and transfix but the animation of the characters within the context that they appear. As a collection of illustrations, the *Fabrica* is presented as a tale of mortality, a story that is told by the body.

As noted above, the skeletons and the muscle men are depicted as dynamic actors, whose gestures represent a record of the dialogue between human life and its mortal coil. As Vesalius states in the preface to the *Fabrica*, the study of anatomy is "research in which we recognize the body and the spirit, as well as a certain divinity that issues from a harmony of the two, and finally our own selves (which is the true study of mankind)."[182] This sensitivity to the experience of human existence as both a sublime and destitute state, manifest in both the body and "spirit," is clearly translated through the contrast of images presented: The tall, proud standing skeleton who finds himself later weeping in despair; and the strong poetic posturing of the muscle man juxtaposed with his own flayed and weakened body, barely able to support himself as he leans against a wall. The story of the figures is apparent in their devastation, but the backgrounds that frame each tale also have significance.

To the delight of many, an early twentieth-century German scholar, E. Jackschath,[183] identified the landscapes depicted behind the muscle men as the Euganean Hills not far from Padua. Although one might be tempted to argue that the backgrounds were chosen in relation to the figures themselves, close examination of the backdrops reveals that the landscapes of each plate, when put side by side, create one broad, continuous mural. As there are few distinguishing characteristics between the divided scenes, one could be led to believe that each figure was arbitrarily assigned to its background for purely aesthetic purposes, as some have asserted, and that the temptation to attribute meaning to the landscape was ultimately unjustified.[184] However, if we keep in mind, as Martin Kemp does, that painting and pictorial arts served a largely narrative function throughout the Middle Ages and well into the sixteenth century, then perhaps the supposed meaninglessness of the figures' contexts should be revisited.

For Martin Kemp, the illustrative backdrop speaks to the "grandeur of natural creation"; the backdrops emphasize that, just as nature has engendered humankind, humankind is situated within a civilization that it too has created.[185] Richard Leppert, on the other hand, interprets the background landscape as a "narrative frame that seemingly either accounts for the figures' deaths or alludes to philosophical issues surrounding death."[186] Leppert is particularly interested in the fact that in several instances the "illustrations connect the new science of anatomy to the execution of prisoners."[187] This is perhaps best evidenced by the depiction of the cadaver hung by a noose. Over and over, the viewer is reminded that the knowledge of life rests upon the knowledge of death. Leppert remarks on the *écorché* from the plate of the ninth muscle man:

[He is] shown in back view . . . [and] becomes like us, a viewer; standing on a hill, he surveys an Italianate landscape with a village and gestures as elegantly as the most cultivated of gentlemen while sporting the body of a young Apollo: beautiful man, beautiful body. As viewers we are invited into the image: "Look at this," the *écorché* seems to say, "what a splendid vista." Stripped of his skin, he remains ignorant that our eyes feast instead on his exposed body, a nude made still more naked by the anatomist's striptease. However, art does more in this instance than hide what needs to be hidden; it also compels us to look, and it does, oddly it might seem, by being rather old-fashioned about its illustrating. By setting the *écorché* "back into" a narrative, a conventional mode of representation, the artist hails the viewer not only to look but to contemplate and admire, to the extent that the image still resonates with the pictorial aura that viewers would associate with art and not with "mere" scientific drawing. In other words, one cultural role played by artists on behalf of anatomists was to transfer some of the prestige long associated with art onto the upstart and still suspicious practice of a new science.[188]

For Jonathan Sawday, the spatial relationship between the figures and their backdrop is the most telling. Also using the example of the muscle men, Sawday suggests that their placement at a distance from the town they observe speaks symbolically to their having fled the social world in order "to reside as isolated inhabitants of an Arcadian and idealized world. The city which lies behind them expresses a human world in which they can no longer participate."[189] For Sawday, the figures appear alive but are, nonetheless, aware "of themselves as inhabitants of the community of the dead," thus provoking the viewers to confront, if only at a distance, their own mortality.[190]

The wealth of continuing speculation and debate around the meaning and import of Vesalius's skeletons and muscle men is a tribute to a text that came into being close to five hundred years ago. The degree to which the illustrations of the *Fabrica* have been internalized and interpreted by its audiences remind us that the legacy of Andreas Vesalius, his actual capacity to live on long after being a part of the "community of the dead," is forever tied to the impact that these images continue to make in the curious minds of those who meditate upon them.

vi. *The Printer and His Print Job*

As the endless hours of dissection, observation, drafting, and editing began to bear fruit, the illustrations were sent away in staggered succession, as they were completed, to the next stage of production. The final step in preparing the *Fabrica's* detailed illustrations for print consisted of having the plates cut into woodblocks. There is some debate as to why Vesalius chose to use woodblock cutting over the newer and more precise practice of copper engraving, which had been used by his associates Gemma and Mercator in production of their terrestrial/celestial globe; but for Vesalius, block printing may have appeared beneficial because it allowed for the densely illustrated text to be printed in a single press run. Woodblock cuts produce a raised or relief surface that allows each woodblock to be inked and printed on the same *forme* as the type fonts. Copper engravings, on the other hand, produced grooves in the metal that held the ink (a method called *intaglio*); each plate thus required a second printing *forme* to be set up for each illustrated page. The extra care required to properly align and register the illustrations with the written text would not only be laborious and extremely time-consuming, but in the end, also prohibitively expensive. Another reason that Vesalius likely chose woodblock plates was the convenient fact that many of the finest block-cutter artisans in Europe worked in Venice. Given the consistent excellence of the *Fabrica* prints, it is reasonable to assume that Vesalius preferred to work with the elite woodblock artisans.

Each woodblock was prepared from pear wood, used because of its very fine grain structure. Each block was sawed in the direction of the grain, sanded until smooth, and then rubbed with linseed oil to soften the surface, which allowed the wood to receive the finest of cuts. The skill of the Venetian cutters also enabled them to taper their cuts and produce fine lines and shading that compared favorably with copper engraving. The volume of the work and the painstaking precision required to produce woodblocks made this a prodigious undertaking.

Commissioning and paying for the woodblocks was a huge expense for Vesalius, and he may have looked for funding from his supporters, among them, his friend Wolfgang Peter Herwart, who had previously offered to assist Vesalius in any way that he could.[191] But this is not certain. Commissioning the block cutting himself, Vesalius closely oversaw the work to ensure that the end product was aligned with his vision. In a letter to the *Fabrica's* printer, Johannes Oporinus, Vesalius discussed at great length how to ensure the integrity of the blocks and how best to avoid their being plagiarized or duplicated. Because of this letter, historians know how the blocks were shipped and who took them, although the cutter(s) remain unknown. Vesalius wrote to Oporinus:

> You will soon receive with this letter, by way of Milanese merchants, the Danoni, the wood blocks engraved for my books *De humani corporis Fabrica* and their *Epitome*. I hope they will be delivered to Basel as safe and sound as when I packed them lest they be damaged in any way, or their transport cause harm. In this I was aided by the meticulous engraver and by Nicolaus Stopius, the trustworthy business agent of the Bombergs here, a young man with a first-class humanistic education.[192]

Due to the craftsmanship of the landscape blocks, it has been speculated that the artisan behind the image, and perhaps the cutting, was a student of Titian's workshop, Campagnolo. Though the certain identity of the "meticulous engraver" has been lost, his outstanding work—the numerous engraved pear woodblocks—survived for many centuries, enabling a 1934 publication of the illustrations to printed using the original blocks. This project helped to ensure that the illustrations of the *Fabrica* would remain forever a part of recorded history. Tragically, these original blocks, the last remains of the original images used to create the *Fabrica*, were destroyed during the bombing of Munich in World War II.

With so much unknown about the artists of the *Fabrica*, there is a temptation to be distracted from the individual who envisioned the project in its entirety. Andreas Vesalius's vision for his magnum opus was a response, not only to the discoveries of his research, but to his recognition of the central importance of illustration and its potential as a medium for education and instruction. As an artistic endeavor by a group of talented artisans, the *Fabrica* remains the material testimony to a unique collaboration in the history of art and medicine, where nuanced representations and procedural text combined to reveal the existential plight of humanity as negotiated by the human body.

Johannes Oporinus,[193] the illustrious print master, was born in Basel in 1507. His given surname was Herbst, meaning "autumn" in German. Consequently, in the humanist tradition of choosing a classical name for oneself, he selected Oporinus, based on an epigram from the Roman poet Martial: "Were Autumn to give me my name, I should be Oporinus." Oporinus's father was a painter from whom he may have acquired an interest and aptitude for design and aesthetics; however, scholarship, not art, was his primary interest as a young man. Having studied Latin and Greek in Strasbourg, Oporinus returned to the University of Basel, where he took various teaching positions.

During the early sixteenth century, Basel was a leading intellectual center, particularly in relation to northern humanist thought and reformist theology. Not only had Erasmus spent the last decades of his life collaborating with his distinguished publisher, Froben, in Basel, but other distinguished intellects, including Amerbach and Herwagen, also came from all over Europe to participate in the progressive discourse and reap the rewards of the new printing and publishing industry. Among the city's beneficiaries was Oporinus. Thomas Plater, a peasant turned scholar, recalls in his autobiography that "Dr. Oporinus" begged and bothered him for Hebrew lessons to such distraction that he eventually submitted and for one hour, one afternoon, took leave of his rope-making duties to educate the doctor personally. Arriving at St. Leonhardt's School, dressed in his dirty work apron, Plater found that Oporinus had assembled eighteen additional students eager to learn.

In addition to his Hebrew, Latin, and Greek studies, Oporinus also studied law and medicine. For several years, Oporinus was the student, secretary, and sometime research subject of Paracelsus, the town physician, eccentric scientist, and "alternative" medical doctor. Though a trying experience, Oporinus's extended internship with the unconventional doctor provided him with an extensive repertoire of medical terminology. Of particular relevance to Vesalius's own beliefs was that Paracelsus had outright dismissed the works of Galen and urged other physicians to use their own sensory perception to determine patients' diseases. In one incident, he is said to have shouted, "[B]urn the authorities!" before taking copies of traditional texts and throwing them onto a fire. Though Oporinus grew to loathe Paracelsus for his drunkenness and excesses, he nonetheless became convinced of the necessity of firsthand observation in the pursuit of scientific knowledge.

In 1533, Oporinus became a professor of Latin at the Pedagogium, the liberal arts college at the University of Basel, and a professor of Greek in 1537. Around the same time, Oporinus established a printing workshop with partners Thomas Plater, Balthasar Ruch, and Robert Winter. The idea of owning and operating a print workshop first occurred to Oporinus and Plater when they were together employed to proof *formes* at Herwagen's workshop. In cooperation with their "good companion," Balthasar Ruch, a skilled and ambitious typesetter with an entrepreneurial spirit, and Oporinus's brother-in-law, Robert Winter, who had the funding and business sense to run the press, the shop was officially opened.

Traditionally, the role of subsidizing print production and distribution fell to the "publisher," in this case, Winter. According to Plater, the real reason Winter agreed to join the other partners was because his wife,

Oporinus's sister, held much of the investment capital herself and was happy to become "a publisher's wife, for she saw the printer's women live in such splendor, for which she was well fitted."[194] As Winter was likely the financial backing to Vesalius's second printing of the *Paraphrase*, only his name, not the press, is credited for its printing.

By taking over an existing printing operation, the partners managed to launch their own business almost immediately. But once they had acquired the printing workshop and all of its equipment from Andrew and Polycarp Cratander (a father-and-son team who were leaving the printing business to become full-time booksellers), the partners found themselves in the tough business of turning a profit. Money was tight. As they struggled to pay for printing supplies, the wages of their journeymen printers, and the exotic new market wares that their wives demanded, tensions inevitably grew among the partners.

With the approach of the most important event of the year, Frankfurt's Great Fair—where booksellers from across Europe went to sell and acquire books—the need for completed manuscripts ready for sale was causing the freshman press significant strain. The shop was producing excellent work; however, it was not prospering. And as time passed, their debt grew rather than diminished. As Plater and Ruch worked late into the night one Sunday evening, their financial situation weighed heavy on one: Plater was proofing the prints, while Ruch oversaw the operation of the press. Always a stickler for accuracy (like Oporinus), Plater sent back one page too many for correction. The normally reserved, Ruch, flew into a rage and shouted "evil words" at Plater, "whatever one does, it is never enough." When Plater retaliated, Ruch seized a board and snuck up behind him, intending to strike. Fortunately, Plater turned in time and blocked the blow with his arms. In the aftermath of this and lesser confrontations, the partnership dissolved. Not surprisingly, Ruch was the first to leave, followed by Winter. In the end, Oporinus was left the sole owner of the operation.

Shifting the focus of the business toward his area of scholarly expertise, Oporinus learned to produce editions of classical texts for which there was increasing demand. As a man of intellect and academic appreciation, he had become known for the educated risks he took in his publication choices. For example, in 1541 Oporinus began production on Theodor Bibliandrus's Latin translation of the Koran. (Bibliandrus was the scholar who had taught Plater Hebrew grammar and whose text was used to tutor Oporinus.) The question of whether producing a translation of the Koran constituted heresy was brought before the Basel city council on the grounds that the Pope himself had ordered the burning of an Arabic translation of the Koran just a few years earlier. Oporinus was found guilty and imprisoned despite his appeal to their reason. Oporinus could have remained in jail indefinitely had not Martin Luther intervened, supporting both the scholar and his decision to publish the Koran. Luther argued that access to the Koran "could only resound 'to the glory of Christ,' the best of Christianity, the disadvantage of the Moslems, and the vexation of the Devil."

Under the skillful charge of Oporinus, the press released the vanguard publications of most of Vesalius's work. The year 1542 would find Oporinus, known for his meticulous attention to detail and refined printing skills, embarking on what would be his most recognized project, the printing and publishing of *Fabrica* and *Epitome* by his "very dear friend" Vesalius.

In August of 1542, Vesalius, his engraver, and his assistant Nicolaus Stropius, the Venice business agent for the Bomberg merchants, packed up the completed woodblocks and proof sheets for the *Fabrica* and *Epitome* in preparation for shipping them from Venice, Italy, to the printer in Basel, Switzerland. With the book's more than four hundred illustrations, a great deal of time and money had gone into the production of the wealth of woodblocks, thus the packing of these blocks for shipping became a critical and painstaking business. Not only were the blocks and proofs themselves vulnerable to damage through handling and weather, but the risk of damage was exasperated by the means of transporting the packing crate. It is not certain which route Vesalius's treasure followed, nor whether it traveled by pack animal, cart, or both, but the most common route from Venice to Basel traversed the Alps via St. Gotthard's Pass and the Devil's Bridge. Despite being one of Europe's busiest trade routes, the mountain pass could accommodate only foot or pack-animal traffic, not carts or wheeled vehicles.

Entrusted with the responsibility of guaranteeing the crate's safe passage, Danoni, a highly regarded Milanese merchant firm, ensured that the production of the text would ensue as planned. The printer, Johannes Oporinus, was by training a classical philologist, and thus was well versed both in the classical languages and literary scholarship. That Vesalius would risk such a precarious trip with his life's work testifies to Oporinus's reputation as a printer of international repute. Although Venice was home to many esteemed scholarly printers, including the Giunta Press, Oporinus's printing workshop was decidedly unique. Vesalius had always turned to Oporinus when he needed quality work for his publications. He would not take any risks with the *Fabrica*.

It is believed that Vesalius's materials arrived in late October of 1542. Accompanying the engraved blocks and prints, Vesalius included a letter requesting structural changes to the publishing plan, indicating that he and Oporinus had previously corresponded over the nature of the texts. Although Oporinus could not have started production of the manuscript until the arrival of the woodblocks, it is likely that he and Vesalius had agreed on certain qualities relating to the text's size, type of paper, and illustrations. Having agreed on some critical details of production, Oporinus was able to make some preliminary provisions before the blocks' arrival and the start of printing.

Having been given sabbatical from Padua, Vesalius was free to travel to Basel around January of 1543 to check on the work that had already begun. The city of Basel, then as today, lay at the intersection of three countries, what are now Switzerland, Germany, and France.[195] Located on the Rhine, Basel was Switzerland's only river port, and ancient trade routes from the Low Countries and the German estates flowed through Basel to the alpine passes leading to Italy and southern Europe. Although the Swiss states had previously been part of the Holy Roman Empire, the revolt of several fifteenth-century Swiss provinces gave rise to the establishment of the Swiss Confederacy. Within the Confederacy, individual states remained independent, differing to varying degrees in their politics and religious leanings. Although the Basel government of the 1540s remained nominally Catholic, it was nonetheless tolerant of, if not sympathetic to, Lutheran and Reformist philosophy and scholarship. It thus provided a wealth of stimulation and intellectual freedom to intellectuals drawn to, among other resources, the city's prolific and infamous printing industry.

Upon arriving in Basel, Vesalius proofed and made minor changes to the *Fabrica*'s pages as they were prepared and printed. Having detailed his expectations for the manuscript, Vesalius left the process of actually printing the text in the capable hands of Oporinus and his workshop staff. On the four hundredth anniversary of the *Fabrica*'s publication in 1943, Carl Rollins, the printer of Yale University Press, spoke at an event sponsored by the Yale University School of Medicine. In his address, Rollins offered an informed reflection on the task that Oporinus had before him. The process of printing the *Fabrica* consisted of a series of laborious tasks: Before composition could begin, *type* would have to be cast, and as Rollins explained, a good typecaster would require two days to craft the specified *type* for each page; then a good compositor, working for a minimum of five hours on each page, would set and assemble each line of type, letter by letter, before placing it in the *forme*. With several hundred pages of text, several compositors would have been employed to complete this stage of production. Once the page *formes* were set and proofed, pages were printed on each side, folded into *folios* (four-page sections), and collected into twelve-page gatherings. All told, the printing of a four-hundred-page text would have amounted to a difficult and exhausting exercise.

When establishing the size of the *Tabulae* sheets, Vesalius decided on large pages (19 by 13.5 inches) so that small anatomical details could be seen clearly and the images could be adopted as presentational tools. In the size of the *Fabrica* pages, we see once again the use of large plates but at a practical, more manageable size, (17 by 11.5 inches), to accommodate both the presentation of detailed illustrations, as well as the extensive text-based expositions. Due to the size and scope of the manuscript, the printing of the *Fabrica* promised to be a costly endeavor and would necessitate selling the final product at a price that fell outside the range of possibility for most students and the general public. It thus stands to reason that the text's intended audience was limited to an elite group of physicians, university libraries, aristocrats, and other well-to-do individuals who could afford to indulge in their curiosities.

Knowing that the *Fabrica* would be too large and expensive to serve as a clinical handbook, Vesalius planned an accompanying publication, the *Epitome*, which he described as "a kind of path" through the books of the *Fabrica*."[196] The *Epitome* appeared both in Latin and German editions in coordination with the publication of the *Fabrica*. It is possible that Vesalius developed the text after completing his work for the *Fabrica*, but the overlap in content indicates that, at least on some level, the two projects were developed together: one, a complete encyclopedic edition of his research and findings, and the other, a practical and accessible text designed to reach as broad an audience as possible. That the two texts were worked on simultaneously is also supported by the fact that the woodcut plates for the *Epitome* were sent to print in Basel alongside those for the *Fabrica*.

With such a large work to contend with, it is likely that some of the printing was contracted out to smaller print shops in Basel. Oporinus had six printing presses, and it would have been difficult, if not impossible, to operate and maintain each simultaneously over the eight to nine months of production. Although there is no documentation to suggest that any of the printing of the *Fabrica* was outsourced, this first edition is marked with a curious and rather noticeable oversight for such a careful printer: a series of page numbers are repeated. Some speculate that the cause of this re-doubling is due to the *Fabrica* having been printed on multiple presses. For example, if multiple print shops were working on the single text simultaneously, an error in pagination might not have been caught in time for publication and could thus have been left uncorrected due to the expense of remedying the mistake. With the exception of some small errors, the production of the *Fabrica* went smoothly, a grace that allowed Vesalius the peace of mind and freedom to remain productive during his stay in Basel.

In the early summer of 1543, while awaiting the completion of the *Fabrica* and *Epitome,* Vesalius found himself introduced to perhaps his career's most colorful subject of dissection.[197] The body was that of a criminal who had previously been apprehended on several capital crime charges, but for unknown reasons, was released shortly after his arrest. Disgusted by her husband's actions, the criminal's wife declined his invitation to move with him to a new district "lest she be implicated in his evil deeds." Despite her refusal to live with him, the wife decided not to divorce her husband in hopes that he would eventually mend his ways. Her husband vanished, and she had not seen him in years until one day he reappeared, walking through the town market with another woman. Astonished, the wife challenged her long-lost spouse, "Good husband, is that woman whom you have with you your wife? Tell me, have you married her? Why are you silent? Why have you turned pale? Why have you dared to add another to your crimes?" The man's companion found voice where he, sputtering denials, had none. "Of course you are," she said to the man. "You married me in church two years ago." The twice-delinquent husband ran off, leaving both women behind.

Shortly following this incident, the husband returned to his first wife, armed with a sword and lance. Hiding along her homeward path, the man savagely attacked the woman and left her for dead. The horror of the act generated a mob of angry citizens who searched out and seized the husband. Found guilty by the senate, the man was condemned to death and beheaded. Following the execution, it was Vesalius's good fortune to dissect the body, and then clean and articulate the skeleton. Today, the Anatomical Institute at the University of Basel houses the articulated skeleton prepared by Vesalius as he awaited his manuscript. Two months following the assault on the unfortunate first wife, Vesalius received the completed unbound manuscript of the *Fabrica*.

vii. *The Royal Edition*

Although the colophon on the last page of the *Fabrica* indicates a publication date of June 1543, it its likely that the actual date was a month or two later. Nonetheless, by late June or early July, Vesalius had managed to acquire a copy of the finished manuscript pages, allowing him to create a unique edition fit to be presented to Emperor Charles V to whom the text was dedicated. Designed to impress, the presentation copy was printed on vellum and "sumptuously bound in purple velvet, with gilt and gauffered edges and four pairs of blue silk ties."[198] The title page and many of the remarkable illustrations within were hand-painted in order to heighten their impact as they reached the eyes of the book's illustrious benefactor.

While Vesalius crafted his dedication, the French king, Francis I, was declaring war on the emperor. On July 10, 1543, French troops invaded Luxembourg and Brabant concurrently. The situation was further aggravated by a former ally of the emperor, the Duke of Cleves, who joined the French military push by invading the Low Countries from the North.[199] Although news of the latest outbreak of war could not have reached Vesalius earlier than late July or early August, it is likely that he was well aware of a general unrest prior to the invasion. This understanding is explicitly evident in a correspondence between the Netherlands' regent, Mary of Hungary, and her brother Charles: "Since the time of our grandfather, the Emperor Maximilian, the Netherlands were never in such danger."[200] Although one could argue that this discernment was limited to those in political positions, as the personal apothecary of the emperor, Vesalius's father's connection to the monarch was an intimate one; thus it is likely that Vesalius too received some correspondence speaking to emerging political tensions.

Vesalius knew firsthand the wrenching effects that war could have. Unlike the 1536 outbreak of Valois-Habsburg hostilities which forced him to leave Paris before completing his medical degree, the latest attack threatened Vesalius's homeland and his family who were likely accompanying the emperor in Spain. The autumn and winter news trickling in from beyond the Alps brought news of escalating attacks. After besieging Antwerp, Marshall Martin van Rossem, the commander for the Guelderland forces of the rebel Duke of Cleves, swept down toward Louvain, setting fire to fields and towns, leaving a path of destruction in his wake. The act of "burning," declared van Rossem, was "the Magnificat of war."[201] But just as Antwerp had resisted the siege, so did the citizens and students of Louvain. Despite inadequate defenses, much of the populace, including students of Louvain, created a front to protect their city. Among these students was Vesalius's friend, Gemma Frisius, who spent four days manning the city walls.

At this time, Charles V was in northern Italy, in Pavia, on his way to southern Germany to lead the front in the war with the French. His strategy was to first subdue the territory of Guelders, which was attacking the Low Countries from the north under the leadership of the turncoat Duke of Cleves. Once he was defeated, the emperor's forces would be directed toward the French. In preparation for the impending campaign, the emperor planned to move to the field encampment of the royal court in southern Germany, not far from Basel. Taking advantage of this close proximity to the emperor, Vesalius set off in early August to present his masterpiece in person.

In a meeting arranged by his father or friends of the court, Vesalius presented the emperor with the royal edition of the *Fabrica*, along with an elegant copy of the *Epitome*, which he had dedicated to Prince Philip, the emperor's son. As there still exist two copies of the *Epitome*, it has been hypothesized that one was presented to the Emperor, while a representative of Vesalius's brought the second copy directly to Prince Philip in Spain, where he was serving as regent in his father's absence. Vesalius had picked a fortuitous moment to present his gift to the monarch. Although he had suffered from gout and other illnesses over the course of the year, Charles V, invigorated by the approaching military campaign and in good health, welcomed the young anatomist and his tribute.

As Vivian Nutton points out, the integration of research and textual discussion with illustrations and other visual representations is today a commonplace phenomenon, particularly in medical and scientific texts. As a result, it is difficult to understand how groundbreaking the *Fabrica* was and the tremendous impact it had on its 1543 audience.[202] Even the emperor, who presumably had been presented with many elaborate illustrated manuscripts before, would never have been witness to such a book as the one presented to him by Andreas Vesalius. Naturally, the same would also be true when the *Fabrica*'s wider audience got its first taste of the long anticipated work.

viii. It's a Gift, It's a Curse

As rumors began to circulate that a maverick scholar was on the verge of releasing an anatomy text that would turn the discipline of medicine on its head, the public's anticipation of the *Fabrica* and *Epitome* was palpable. In the spring of 1543, a professor of medicine at Basel, Hieronymus Gemusaeus, hinted to his colleague that a most significant work was about to be published by Oporinus. On August 1, after having had the good fortune to study the groundbreaking text himself, Hieronymus "hailed Vesalius as the leading figure in the discipline of anatomy" due to his clarifications on Galen and the ingenuity of his discoveries.[203] On August 2, another Basel resident, Johannes Gast, sent copies of the new anatomical work to his friend, Heinrich Bullinger, a leader in the reformist movement, living in Zurich.[204] Vesalius's students also waited feverishly for the arrival of the *Fabrica* and its less expensive companion text, the *Epitome*. Expecting a ready market for both texts, Oporinus released the two simultaneously along with a German translation that was published on August 9.

By all accounts, the sales of Vesalius's masterworks were brisk. The bookseller of Leipzig, for example, sold out of all copies of both the *Fabrica* and the *Epitome* by the end of 1543, forcing such characters of history as the physician and scholar, George Agricola, to order his copies from Frankfurt because all the copies in Leipzig had been sold out.[205] Although this event is itself inconsequential, the fact that seemingly trivial details such as these are recorded for posterity is indicative of their contextual import. In an age when a journey of a few hundred miles might take weeks, the dissemination of the *Fabrica* to its scholarly audience took many months, and to some distant residents, even years, but word of its brilliance spread immediately. It has been recorded that at least three copies of the *Fabrica* were known to be available in Oxford, England, by 1546,[206] evidence not only that interest in Vesalius's work was far-reaching, but also that many years would pass before the full reception of the work was felt by the public and its author.

However long it took the *Fabrica* to arrive, it always found the same reception. The quality and innovation of the text astounded its audience and announced Vesalius immediately as a vanguard scholar across fields and disciplines, including medicine and science, art, printing, and the humanities. Although much of the praise and respect outlined above reflects the *legacy* of the *Fabrica* and its creator, it is important to recall that the content of the *Fabrica* was not well received by all.

Following the completion of the *Fabrica*, Vesalius took to traveling through northern Italy and stopping at various universities along the way to discuss his work and perform anatomical demonstrations. Although his receptions in Padua, Bologna, and Pisa were very positive, he initially experienced hostility from some of the emperor's court physicians. Threatened by Vesalius's experience and insight, and resentful of the emperor's praise of the *Fabrica* and its author, these men attempted to belittle Vesalius before the emperor by challenging the validity of his work. Their efforts were much in vain for Vesalius was well familiar with being the source of controversy.

Throughout his education and in response to his earliest published works, Vesalius recognized that his traditionalist contemporaries did not welcome some of his conclusions. As a student and as a teacher, Vesalius was an adamant proponent of the need for firsthand dissection, and he regularly challenged physicians and scholars who were either steadfast proponents of medieval medical practices or newly converted Galenists. Each insisted on listening only to the authorities of the past and refused to see what was before his eyes. Anticipating the criticism that he would receive from his latest and most extensive challenge to Galenic thought, Vesalius addresses the issue in the *Fabrica*'s preface, noting:

> how doctors (quite unlike the followers of Aristotle) tend to become agitated when it comes to their attention nowadays in the course of a single anatomical demonstration that Galen has departed more than two hundred times from a true description of the harmony, use, and function of the human parts, and they grimly puzzle over the dissected pieces with the utmost determination to defend him.[207]

Vesalius goes on to appeal to these physicians, for the love of truth, to trust their eyes and reason and to put Galen to the test by "returning to the body" through the practice of dissection and sense observation. Only by this method, argued Vesalius, could true anatomical understanding be the foundation of medicine.

While the *Fabrica* immediately persuaded some readers, others were more skeptical of its merits. As expected, the major point of contention for many scholars and medical practitioners was their conviction that Galen was infallible in his observations. As Vesalius wrote:

> These men could not believe that the father of medicine had made such mistakes in the anatomical books he felt he had written with so much care and accuracy, the more so since it was a subject in which he had acquired greater authority than anyone else, even during his own lifetime. Gradually, however, they began to change their attitude, and there was not one among them who, with the cadaver before him, could continue to defend Galen. However reluctantly, they came to put more faith in their own eyes than in the words of Galen.[208]

One of the early mixed reviews of the *Fabrica* appeared in the form of two letters written on January 20 and 22, 1544, by the Venetian physician Nicolo Massa. Massa, like Vesalius, claimed in his 1536 book on anatomy to have performed his own dissections and encouraged others interested in anatomical research to do the same. Unlike Vesalius's efforts, however, Massa's work did not result in many original findings despite his disciplined attention to autopsy. Massa was not critical of Vesalius's corrections of Galen; rather he took offense to Vesalius's neglecting to acknowledge the work of his contemporaries and his not showing adequate respect for teachers and fellow anatomists, such as Massa.[209] As Vesalius had made it very clear that his accomplishments were his own, it is likely that Massa's comments fell on deaf ears.

Among his other detractors, Cornarius, a leading translator of Galen at the University of Marburg, took great offense to Vesalius's take on

Galen and took heavy black ink to his copy of the 1542 Latin edition of Galen's *Opera Galeni*, striking out Vesalius's name wherever it appeared and boldly correcting what he perceived as impious mistakes. John Caius, who coedited the same edition with Vesalius, made similar corrections of language in his copy of the 1541 edition.

During the early years after the *Fabrica*'s publication, the most vehement and disturbing criticism came from Vesalius's professor from the University of Paris, Jacobus Sylvius. Shortly after the *Fabrica*'s publication, Vesalius was asked to send an introductory letter to several professors in Paris's Faculty of Medicine on behalf of a friend's son who had recently been accepted into the program. In his letter to Sylvius, Vesalius later recalled that in addition to the accolades he relayed about Jaochim Roelant's son, he had also suggested that:

> if any comments in my books on anatomy had displeased him, I hoped he would tell me what they were. For I thought it concerned him, too, if I published anything, since he had established among his colleagues such a high reputation in anatomy, and since I had begun studying medicine with him.[210]

Although Sylvius had not yet read Vesalius's latest work, he nonetheless responded to the invitation with a highly critical letter objecting to Vesalius's analysis of Galen. When Vesalius wrote back asking for further explanation, Sylvius replied that what disturbed him most was Vesalius's assertion that Galen had only dissected two human bodies and that his anatomical descriptions were based primarily on the dissection of animals and only superficial observations of the human body. Sylvius then proceeded to suggest that he would generously not slander him during his own anatomy lectures and would resist encouraging his students to formally and publicly criticize him, if only Vesalius would withdraw his "false statements" about Galen and attribute them to youthful error. As one would expect, Vesalius categorically declined Sylvius's offer.

Though they may have ceased to continue a personal correspondence, Vesalius and Sylvius continued to argue with much venom over various points of disagreement. As will be discussed shortly, Vesalius responded to Sylvius's criticisms within his 1546 publication *Letter on the China Root*. In response, Sylvius challenged Vesalius (though not by name) in his 1546 edition of Galen's *On the Bones*, asserting that Galen's original text was based solely on the study of human bones. As the years passed and the success of the *Fabrica* grew far beyond what Sylius could stomach, he finally published a direct attack on Vesalius in the 1551 publication, *Vaesani cuiusdam calumniarum in Hippocratis Galenique rem anatomicam dupulsio* (*A Refutation of the Slanders of a Madman against the Anatomy of Hippocrates and Galen*). The word *vaesani*, "madman," was an obvious play on Vesalius's name. True to its title, Sylvius's text liberally attacks Vesalius, calling him "the insolent and ignorant slander who . . . treasonably attacked his teachers with violent mendacity time and again distorted the truth of nature."

To Sylvius, Vesalius was "a mad deserter" of the Galen tradition, which enraged and embittered him to such a degree that he called upon the emperor personally to:

> punish severely, as he deserves, this monster born and bred in his own house, this worst example of ignorance, ingratitude, arrogance, and impiety, to suppress him so that he may not poison the rest of Europe with his pestilential breath. He has already infected certain Frenchmen, Germans, and Italians with his deadly exhalation, but only those ignorant of anatomy and the rest of medicine. If they had acquired even a cursory knowledge of these subjects by reading Galen's books, or, even better, by undertaking or at least observing many anatomies, they would never have been so foolish as to leave their own excellent leaders so hastily for the camp of ignorance.[211]

The great irony of Sylvius's polemic, of course, was that he argued that the truth of Galen could only be reinstated through firsthand dissection, precisely Vesalius's practice and personal philosophy.

Although studies of his teachings and medical practice suggest that Sylvius was not so rigid a Galenist as his attacks on Vesalius suggest, he did have a deep professional and personal investment in Galen's authority. Like other humanist scholars, his linguistic scholarship was directed at restoring Galen to a classical age of reverence and authority. Sylvius was considered an outstanding anatomist in his own right whose research contributed greatly to anatomical education and Galenic scholarship; however, his public vendetta against Vesalius eventually tarnished his reputation.

In several instances, Sylvius and other anatomists who objected to Vesalius's observations and corrections of Galen, claimed that while performing their own dissections, they had many times observed the structures that Vesalius had insisted did not exist. Sylvius, for instance, continued to claim that he had observed the minute pores in the walls dividing the chambers of the heart. Whether these anatomists really did see what they hoped to see, or if they were merely trying to contradict Vesalius is unknown, but the truth is likely a mix of both. Even Vesalius himself continued to "see" structures that Galen had said existed in the human body—when in reality they did not.

Sylvius's obsession with disgracing Vesalius's reputation began to affect, among other things, the quality of his teaching, as described in an account by Renatus Henerus, a student of Sylvius's at the University of Paris.

> While Sylvius was in labor with [the Vaesanus], as I now realize, we were forced to endure a constant stream of abuse and virtually incessant and furious invective against Vesalius. It wearied our ears and aroused the indignation of many of us.[212]

Henerus attributed Sylvius's hatred of Vesalius in part to the fact that the publication of the *Fabrica* preceded and thus forestalled Sylvius's publication of his own general anatomy text. This book, the *Isogoge*, had been completed as early as 1542 but would not be published until after Sylvius's death in 1555. Although it is inevitable that the story between Sylvius and his ex-student has blurred over the centuries, what does seem true is that Sylvius's animosity toward Vesalius ultimately discredited him to many a student and colleague alike.

Of course, not all received the *Fabrica* with cynicism and bitterness. By the late 1540s and early 1550s, the tide of anatomical study had begun to move toward direct observation through the practice of dissection, leading many of the open-minded to the discoveries that Vesalius's publication was presenting. As the first public review of the *Fabrica* by Hieronymus Gemusaeus suggests,[213] there was indeed a community that stood behind Vesalius and saw his achievements as marvelous. Contrary to seeing Vesalius as a heretic, Gemusaeus, who had himself edited a Greek edition of Galen's collected works in 1538, saw Vesalius's dedication to anatomical inquiry as evidence that he was a true follower of the spirit of Galen. Gemusaeus viewed Vesalius's work, not as a rejection of Galen, but as a respectful and proper response to Galen's own assertions and goals as they pertained to the study of anatomy. Although the *Fabrica* represented a break with the past for many scholars, the work remained solidly within the framework of Galenic medicine and anatomy. This is evidenced in Gemusaeus's praise of Vesalius for having uncovered and recounted passages from Galen that had been previously unknown to most sixteenth-century practitioners.[214]

Well beyond medical circles, the *Fabrica* also attracted interest from the Lutheran reformer, Melanchthon, who pored over his copy of Vesalius's text, closely reading and annotating every page. So taken with the *Fabrica* was he that he wrote a poem in praise of it on the inside cover of his copy. Additionally, in the 1551 revision of his own book, *On the Soul*[215]—a required text in Lutheran schools and universities—Melanchthon praised Vesalius and incorporated many of the *Fabrica*'s findings within its pages.

Across Europe, many humanist physicians recognized in the *Fabrica* a clear articulation of an emerging change in the field of anatomy. No previous publication had so extensively or critically outlined Galen's anatomy or detailed it so radically through the use of illustration; and many who taught anatomy—such as Realdo Colombo, Vesalius's substitute at Padua and Leonhard Fuchs, the famous botanist who taught medicine at the University of Tübingen—immediately began to use the findings of the *Fabrica* in their own teachings. Vesalius and his masterwork had become the inspiration for many others' success.

Perhaps Realdo Columbo was tired of being constantly reminded of his predecessor's preeminence, or perhaps he had a firm conviction of his own prowess, but for whatever reason, Colombo not only incorporated Vesalius's discoveries and observations into his own teaching but he also immediately began to boast that he himself could identify anatomical structures that remained unknown to Vesalius. When Vesalius returned unexpectedly to Padua in the autumn of 1543, he was displeased to hear of Colombo's groundless claims. Uncharacteristically, Vesalius took his revenge three years later by describing Colombo in print as a man "who learned something of anatomy by assisting me in my work, although he was incompletely educated."[216] Vesalius's frustration was likely exasperated when, soon after his visit to Padua, he learned that Colombo had been offered and had accepted a professorship at Pisa after Vesalius was forced to turn the position down. Colombo's actions in Padua were arrogant and self-serving, but to his credit, he was an able dissector and anatomist. Thus it is conceivable that the *Fabrica*'s achievement spurred him to advance his own studies. After three years in Pisa, Colombo moved to the University of Rome where he remained for the rest of his life. In 1559, a year after his death, his only published work, *De re anatomica* (*On Things Anatomical*) appeared in print, and it remained one of the best introductions to anatomy for many years afterward.

In Germany, Leonhard Fuchs, an internationally prominent physician, was also very impressed with the *Fabrica*. In 1542, the year prior to the *Fabrica*'s publication, Fuchs published one of the period's most important and beautiful books on botany, a realistic and lavishly illustrated herbal atlas. After the *Fabrica* and *Epitome* came into his hands, Fuchs began to adopt Vesalius's work within his own medical instruction for he felt that anatomy was much neglected in Germany. Sometime before 1551, Fuchs began to plan an anatomical work that would fulfill what he perceived to be pedagogical need.

> [W]ith the exception of the commentaries of our Vesalius
> on the structure of the human body, clearly learned and
> produced with remarkable industry, I have discovered

no writing that has satisfied me entirely and that I could use suitably for the discussion of the human body and its dissection.[217]

Fuchs found Vesalius's publications, even as excellent as they were, to be ultimately unsuitable for the classroom: the *Fabrica* was too long to be practical, and the *Epitome* was insufficient in its brevity. Additionally, he felt that the *Fabrica* was not adequately accessible to the mass of German medical professors who were largely unskilled in anatomy. Therefore, after years of using his own interpretive writings on Galen in combination with Vesalius's commentary, Fuchs decided that, in response to his students' wishes, he would prepare a manuscript of his own. The purpose of his "epitome," Fuchs claimed, was:

> to prepare a pathway for the reader for an easier understanding of Vesalius [who] was divinely inspired to recall into the light and make known this part of medicine that was almost extinct and contaminated with infinite errors.[218]

Among those anatomists most inspired by Vesalius, Gabriele Fallopio would in turn assume a position of equal import and influence in Vesalius's work. Early in his career, Fallopio studied at Ferrara where he enjoyed the friendship of Giovanni Baptista Canano, who was also Vesalius's friend. As a physician, Fallopio had taught at Ferrara and then assumed Colombo's position at Pisa. In 1551, he took the chair of anatomy at Padua. Fallopio was a "spiritual disciple" of Vesalius's, and he honored Vesalius by making the *Fabrica* the foundation for his own research and work. In 1561 he published *Observationes anatomicae* (*Anatomical Observations*), which is both a critical commentary on the *Fabrica* and a presentation of Fallopio's own discoveries and observations. Vesalius's last published work would be in response to Fallopio's *Observationes*.

Though one could argue that anatomists like Fallopio, Fuchs, and Colombo were developing their own careers on the back of Vesalius's work, it is important to remember that Vesalius's achievement was in creating a clearing in the dense and obscurant growth of centuries of traditional and speculative anatomical theory. As the *Fabrica* effectively charted this new terrain for its audience, it became impossible for anatomists, physicians, and scholars to ignore it. Even where Vesalius was completely omitted from an anatomy treatise proposed by one of his detractors, this exclusion nonetheless constituted his inclusion because it positioned the author clearly as an anti-Vesalian. In this way, all anatomy that followed Vesalius had to deal with him in some capacity. In fact, the field of anatomy in the era preceding the *Fabrica* is today commonly referred to as "pre-Vesalian anatomy."

In trying to understand the basic issues between Vesalius and his contemporaries, it is useful to understand the vast spectrum of criticism against him, for not all scholars had the same things at stake in his work. The central issues among anatomy scholars related to points of interpretation and textual research, and whether or not it was heretical to look to verify the sacred truths of classical authors. In terms of scholarship, Vesalius's most vocal critics argued that he did not possess an adequate aptitude for Greek translation and that the Greek manuscripts, the Latin translations of which Vesalius relied upon for his research, were inherently flawed and of poor quality. (Although these scholars' assessment of the texts was justified to a degree, several centuries of continued textual scholarship has found that "improvements [in translations] have been in details rather than in any overall conception or level of accuracy on the part of Galen."[219]). The distain of those who challenged Vesalius's undermining of Galenic medicine was largely focused on his assertion that Galen had not based his research on dissected human bodies, and they dismissed Vesalius altogether. To this community of unrest, Sylvius added that, if some anatomical parts of the modern human were different from those described by Galen, then it was likely an indication of a decline and change in human anatomy since the time of Galen and not proof that he had based his work on the study of animals. Though a theory presumably born out of desperation, five years of critical observations by Charles Darwin three hundred years later would develop a theory that would have allowed Sylvius to argue his position a bit more soundly, however erroneous it would have remained.

For Sylvius and scholars like him, hands-on anatomy marked the restoration of a distant authority and a return to an age of superior knowledge. But for Vesalius, Colombo, Canano, Fallopio, Fabriscius, Eustachio, and a host of other anatomists from the mid-sixteenth century onward, dissection was an answer to Galen's call to return to the body as the source by which anatomical knowledge could be verified and expanded. Although it would take many decades for Vesalius's approach to be widely accepted by some of his more conservative contemporaries—through attrition as much as by insight—a progressive comportment towards Galenic doctrine and the practice of empirical study of the body through dissection became the increasingly accepted methodology of anatomical inquiry.

From the first published scholarly critiques of the *Fabrica* appearing in late 1543, until his death in 1564, debate ensued as to whether Vesalius was the start or the end of anatomical study. Though the debate has been described by some as more "bluster than storm," the rancor and hostile jibes made by some Galenists disturbed, troubled, and gnawed at Vesalius's soul.[220]

CHAPTER SEVEN

An Imperial Appointment

In the preface to the *Fabrica*, Vesalius asserts that the primary value of medical research and knowledge was in its application as a healing art. Although he may have indirectly considered this the founding ideal of his life's work, he had previously shown himself to be formally an academic with little experience as a physician. From the onset of Vesalius's academic life, he had been able to focus single-mindedly on his studies, research, and writing; but upon his acceptance into the court of Emperor Charles V, Vesalius would find that his life was becoming altogether different than what he had expected.

i. Vesalius Goes to War

While Oporinus worked to distribute the *Fabrica* around Europe, the autumn of 1543 saw Vesalius fulfill the destiny of his family name. Following the presentation of the royal edition of the *Fabrica* to Emperor Charles V, Vesalius was immediately offered the post of *medicus familiaris ordinaries,* regular physician to the household, within the Emperor's Royal Court. As was the convention of the time, Vesalius's dedication to the emperor was a means of securing professional promotion. As the secular and ecclesiastical courts of Europe were the primary sources of patronage for the arts and sciences, and since patronage was the surest route to prestige and financial security, Vesalius's success allowed him to either remain a professor of medicine at a prominent university or to seek the privilege of an invitation into imperial service. In dedicating his masterwork to the emperor, Vesalius followed through with the choice that had effectively been made for him by four generations of the van Wesele family.

Vesalius would be the physician to the emperor for more than thirteen years. Prone to numerous illnesses, Charles kept many physicians within his court with whom he consulted for diagnosis and treatment. Historians have debated the degree of prestige and breadth of responsibility associated with Vesalius's imperial position; however, it is clear that Vesalius never held the prestigious position of primary physician to the emperor, nor was he permitted liberty to be released from service.

In early 1543, prior to Vesalius's *Fabrica* dedication and presentation, Charles V had appointed Cornelius van Baersdorp as his primary body physician, a post which he continued to serve in until the emperor's death in Spain in 1558. Dr. Baersdorp was born to an illustrious family from the Netherlands, yet he was not as well known or well regarded as young Andreas Vesalius. This was of no consequence to the emperor who, despite his reverence for the young anatomist, never promoted him to a rank higher than second in the hierarchy of his court physicians. In fact, Vesalius's first duty as a physician of the court took him far from the emperor's side and placed him securely under the wing of another physician, Daza Chacon. Having long preached that the primary purpose of medical study was to influence the practice of the healing arts, Vesalius was about to be put to the test.

For most of Vesalius's life, the reign of Charles V and his son Phillip II was characterized by military conflict and political unrest. In addition to the war between the Royal Empire and France, domestic struggles between the Lutheran reformists and Catholic Church incited further conflict within the Low Countries. From the distant gaze of present times, the conflicts and issues of the sixteenth century are assumed to have been between nations, and consequently, we speak of conflicts between England and France, France and Spain, or France and the Empire. But in truth the major powers acting on the European stage were dynastic entities, reflecting conflicts between families and economic interests more than national identities and freedoms.[221] In the war of ideas, Vesalius had become well-schooled and had faced opposition many times from those who perceived his return to Galen's mandate for empirical knowledge as an act of betrayal. But as a military physician, Vesalius found himself in the midst of conflict unlike anything he had experienced before. In war he would see with his own eyes, through the "hand's work in healing," what his training had only partially prepared him for.

On the verge of the campaign to retake Guelders, a duchy of the Low Countries, Charles V sent Vesalius to the front to provide care for the emperor's commanders, who were leading the operation. During the sixteenth century, surgeons were not formally attached to the military. Thus, during times of conflict, noble commanders and their officers dispersed many of their own medical attendants to assist in the field. Although the physicians and surgeons of the royal court were primarily responsible for the care of their sovereign, it was the emperor's prerogative to utilize their skills wherever he saw fit, even in the chaos of battle.

In the campaign for Guelders, Vesalius received an education far different than what his texts and cadavers had shown him. Daza Chacon, for all intents and purposes, was both Vesalius's friend and teacher in the battlefield. An experienced and practical surgeon, Chacon observed and recorded Vesalius's early training and difficulties and marked his progress as his skills evolved. In essence, much of Vesalius's training in the field is best characterized as a trial by fire. The appearance of previously unseen wounds and injuries received by soldiers on the battlefield forced physicians to experiment with treatments and therapeutic practices. For example, the recent adoption of small firearms in battle raised particular challenges for surgeons. At the time, many physicians believed that the bullets and extraneous material carried into bodies from gunshots "poisoned" the wounds; thus in order to clean them, patients' sores were cauterized with hot oil or hot irons, and then packed with various preparations. Unfortunately, these therapies added more debris to sores and further traumatized the damaged tissues and patients. As the infected gunshot wounds festered and worsened, it was not unusual for gangrene to set in, forcing radical amputations to be performed. Although the noted French surgeon, Ambroise Paré, and other physicians such as Bartolomeo Maggi were independently concluding that less invasive treatments led to better results, it was not be until Paré's 1545 publication on the subject that such alternative treatments became generally adopted.

Other devastating and grievous wounds experienced by soldiers and treated by field surgeons included those incurred by artillery and pikes. These were conventionally treated through the suturing and cauterizing of lacerations or, when wounds were too extensive, limb amputations. For Vesalius, having to perform these extreme procedures on living patients proved to be considerably more difficult than were the demands of his previous experience with oblivious cadavers. Not only were the injuries more extensive than what he had previously seen in postmortem examinations, but without effective anesthetics, treatments had to be completed quickly and proficiently on conscious and writhing patients. As a battlefield surgeon, Vesalius was not an immediate success. Chacon observed that during one of Vesalius's first stints on the battlefield, despite his skills of autopsy and dissection, he struggled to amputate an arm at the elbow. Although Chacon recognized Vesalius's initial awkwardness, he later reported instances in which Vesalius independently, or in collaboration with Daza, developed original surgical procedures.

By the end of October 1543, the campaign for Guelders was concluded with the surrender of the Duke of Cleves. Anticipating an engagement with King Francis's forces, Charles turned his services south toward Artois. But as winter set in, the looming conflict was postponed, with each side preferring to retreat and prepare for spring campaigns. With the army in winter quarters and with his position within the emperor's court not yet formalized, Vesalius received permission to return to Italy to conduct a series of anatomy demonstrations at the newly reopened University of Pisa. That Charles V granted Vesalius leave was likely a political move, not personal one, as the Emperor wanted to bolster his support for the young Duke of Tuscany, Cosimo de Medici. The Duke, it seems, was very much involved with arranging Vesalius's visit and would later beseech the emperor to free the reluctant court physician from his imperial service.

ii. Slings and Arrows

In December of 1543, Vesalius returned to Italy and to the University of Padua. Although his visit appears to have been relatively unexpected, their surprise was marginal relative to Vesalius's shock at finding his professorial substitute, Realdo Colombo, "industriously belittling his reputation" in his absence.[222] As mentioned earlier, Colombo had been Vesalius's student and assistant and was formally acknowledged for his work in the *Fabrica*; but upon his return to Padua, Vesalius discovered that Colombo was claiming to have surpassed his former mentor: "[W]hile I was absent from Padua, [Columbo] dissected a body and boasted that he had found something that was unknown to me." Although Colombo would become a famous anatomist himself and contribute genuinely to the field, he was also known for his affinity for exaggeration and hyperbole.

If Colombo had indeed been working to undermine Vesalius's reputation, then his attempts proved to be in vain. The Paduan authorities welcomed Vesalius and immediately asked him to lecture and perform the upcoming public anatomy demonstrations before he continued on to Bologna and Pisa. Naturally, Vesalius accepted. Crammed into the small temporary theater, audiences of more than five hundred jockeyed to observe the famous imperial surgeon at work. The novelty and excitement surrounding the event were further amplified by the fact that the cadaver to be dissected was the body of a young female, which the students of the school had snatched from a tomb by the Church of San Antonio. The rare specimen was ideal for the body was that of a beautiful, young prostitute. Vesalius reported that her body was particularly suited for dissection, because it was slightly emaciated. He also noted that the cause of her death, inflammation of the azygos vein and thorax, would give him the unique opportunity to demonstrate the condition of pleurisy.

Having completed the public demonstrations, Vesalius left Padua sometime after December 28. In the company of a Pisan physician, Petrus Martyr Tronus, he took the road toward Pisa, stopping along the way at Bologna to visit his old friend Giovanni Andrea Bianchi. It was likely no coincidence that his arrival coincided with Bologna's own winter anatomy demonstrations. Although Bartolomeo Maggi was responsible for the lectures, professor and students alike begged the distinguished anatomist to "dissect the major parts of a body then available."[223] Again, Vesalius agreed and immediately took up the scalpel to painstakingly demonstrate what he felt was most important, the venous system. As he lectured, the extensive performance stretched into the night until finally fatigue and the bitter cold forced an end to his work. Throughout the dissection and lecture, those in attendance refrained from challenging Vesalius or asking questions, believing that the following day would allow for such inquiry. But it did not.

Vesalius was no stranger to Bologna or its conservative ideologies. During his previous series of dissections in 1539, Vesalius found himself in heated debate with many of the faculty, particularly Curtius. Whether Vesalius was facing a time constraint or just wished to avoid a debate, he took his leave in the morning of the next day without any recorded explanation. Later that same morning, a doctrinal debate around the anatomy lecture and dissection broke out, with various parties arguing for their favorite classical authority, Aristotle versus Galen. No one, it seems, grounded his argument in the physical evidence that had been so laboriously presented to the group the day before.

iii. The Madman Cometh

On or around January 22, 1544, Vesalius finally arrived in Pisa. The invitation and acquisition of the master anatomist by Duke Cosimo was an event meant to highlight the integrity of the university and to promote its reopening. For a short time, in the fourteenth century, the University of Pisa had rivaled Padua and Bologna in its academic prowess; however, the Black Death of 1348 dealt the university a severe blow from which it never fully recovered. In the sixteenth century, internal political unrest in Tuscany between the Valois and Habsburg princes forced the university to close its doors until it was renovated and reopened in November of 1543. To bolster the university's status, the duke dispatched a deputy to recruit leading professors in various fields. Vesalius's agreement to conduct a special anatomy demonstration at Pisa was nothing short of a triumph for the school.

Since the school did not know exactly when Vesalius would arrive, most arrangements for the planned dissection could not be made in advance. When Vesalius did arrive, he found that he would have to wait for cadavers to be located, and that the school's stock of bones was grossly insufficient. Wasting no time, the students and the university authorities sprang into action. Having made a set of keys for the Cemetery of San Pisano, the students managed to acquire the necessary bones and "found" the body of a "hunchback girl, who, [Vesalius] conjectured, had died because of an impediment to respiration caused by her malformation."[224] Additionally, the Bishop of Marsico dispatched a letter on the duke's behalf to an advisor in Florence, stating their immediate need for bodies.

> Vesalius has arrived here to conduct his anatomical demonstrations, and his arrival has greatly pleased his Excellency who has ordered that everything be made ready with all dispatch. A courier has been sent especially to procure two cadavers, and his Excellency has ordered me to write to you to inquire in the Hospital of Santa Maria Nuova for bodies of persons young rather than old, although Campana says it is not necessary that they be very young nor that one of them be a woman. When they have been found, let them be enclosed in two cases and sent as quickly as possible down the Arno by barge or boat. This matter ought to be handled by you secretly, both the procurement of those bodies and their dispatch, and let them be delivered to the convent of San Francesco of the conventual friars where everything will be arranged.[225]

It is interesting to note that, although both state and spiritual authorities supported the dissections, extreme care was nonetheless being taken to protect the sensitivities of the local citizenry by procuring cadavers from outside the community and transporting them in secret. Shortly after the first letter was sent, a barge carrying the body of a nun arrived in Pisa. Despite the body being of anatomical interest, Vesalius determined that the woman had not died of pleurisy as suspected, but of another unidentified disease, the deforming effects of which prevented his planned demonstration. The bishop immediately dispatched another letter to Florence, asking for "more human bodies, please, as well as those of animals."[226]

As expected, Vesalius's demonstrations drew large and eager audiences, including the duke, who attended when he could. It was recorded that observers packed the benches so densely, shifting and turning for better vantage points, that at one point a Master Carlo lost his footing, fell from the bench, and injured himself so seriously that he could no longer attend the proceedings. While in Pisa, Vesalius was also called upon to perform the autopsies of at least two prominent citizens: one, a leading jurist, Belloarmato of Siena, and the other, a leading physician, Prospero Martello. The request for assistance came directly from Pisa's resident physicians who were already at work on the bodies but wished to draw from the expertise that Vesalius would bring to the examination.

In contrast to the critical and antiquated intellectual life of Bologna, Pisa welcomed Vesalius's innovation and revolutionary methodology. In fact, he had made such a favorable impression on the medical faculty and the duke that Cosimo had his ambassador petition Emperor Charles V to allow Vesalius to remain in Pisa as a professor at the university at a substantial compensation of 800 crowns. The emperor refused.

It is not known if Vesalius wished to stay in Pisa or return to the imperial court. Since Vesalius did not formally comment on his introduction to military service and because there is no concrete evidence that he had an expressed desire to return to a life of research and scholarship, it is not certain what next step Vesalius wished to take with his life. What is known, however, is that after his dissection tour of Italy, but before he assumed his imperial position within the emperor's court, Vesalius destroyed all of his books, sketches, notes, and papers by throwing them into the fire. This, I argue, was the defining turning point in Vesalius life.

With the burning of all of his life's work, a wealth of research, detailed annotations, translations, and observations were lost forever. Years later,

Vesalius would reflect on this event with deep regret, stating that he had been frustrated that his honest attempt to further his own knowledge of anatomy should be met with such cutting criticisms and personal attacks.

All these impediments I made light of; for I was too young to seek gain by my art, and I was sustained by my eager desire to learn and to promote the studies in which I shared. I say nothing of my diligence in anatomizing—those who attended my lectures in Italy know how I spent three whole weeks over a single public dissection. But consider that in one year I once taught in three different universities. If I had put off the task of writing till this time; if I were now just beginning to digest my materials; students would not have had the use of my anatomical labours, which posterity may or may not judge superior to the rechauffes formerly in use, whether of Mesua, of Gatinaria, of some Stephanus or other on the differences, causes and symptoms of diseases, or, lastly, of a part of Servitor's pharmacopoeia. As to my notes, which had grown into a huge volume, they were all destroyed by me; and on the same day there similarly perished the whole of my paraphrase on the ten books of Rhazes to King Almansor, which had been composed by me with far more care than the one which is prefaced to the ninth book. With these also went the books of some author or other on the formulae and preparation of medicines, to which I had added much matter of my own which I judged to be not without utility; and the same fate overtook all the books of Galen which I had used in learning anatomy, and which I had liberally disfigured in the usual fashion. I was on the point of leaving Italy and going to Court; those physicians you know of had made to the Emperor and to the nobles a most unfavourable report of my books and of all that is published nowadays for the promotion of study; I therefore burnt all these works that I have mentioned, thinking at the same time that it would be an easy matter to abstain from writing for the future. I must show that I have since repented more than once of my impatience, and regretted that I did not take the advice of the friends who were then with me. [227]

It is impossible to determine the magnitude of the loss to sixteenth-century medicine caused by Vesalius's rash action, but whatever this cost may have been, it was nothing relative to what Vesalius lost that day—his life as he knew it. When we talk about the myth that has become Andreas Vesalius, it begins here, for it does not seem reasonable that Vesalius's destructive violence was an act directed to his critics, as he claims above. Rather, the excessive nature of his behavior indicates an extreme personal crisis and a rage directed, not at others, but toward himself.

One should not let the passage of time reduce this radical self-destructive gesture to the level of a mere anecdotal event within Vesalius's life. During the period following the release of the *Fabrica*, Vesalius had indeed been faced with a greater wave of scrutiny and condemnation than he had previously experienced; however, based on his previous participation in fevered debates like those with Sylvius and Curtius it does not follow that Vesalius would be so ill-prepared for the predictable onslaught of disparaging attacks. In fact, when one reads the substance of Vesalius's scathing retorts to his critics, it seems reasonable to surmise that Vesalius even enjoyed this kind of intellectual sparring.

In the classic role of a tragic hero, Vesalius moves down a path clearly laid out by destiny, only to find, at the precise moment when his goal is to be achieved, that what he once desired has become loathsome to him. If we look at this critical period in Vesalius's life, we find a man who, in the publication of the *Fabrica*, has reached the pinnacle of achievement in his work. Vesalius has been rewarded for his efforts with imperial service to Charles V and has fulfilled his familial inheritance by becoming the fifth generation of Wesele to receive such a prestigious invitation. But, unlike his forefathers, Vesalius has made an exceptional and historic contribution to the field of medicine—and, one might suspect, he knows it.

The irony of the *Fabrica*'s publication is that it is at once the culmination of Vesalius's life's work to date and the beginning of the end of (what he sees as) his rightful place in medicine. Upon completion of the *Fabrica*, Vesalius was rewarded by being immediately called away from his scholarly work and pulled into the position of military surgeon. Once in the field, he quickly realized that he was not skilled in the way of applied surgery and felt, perhaps for the first time in his life, incompetent and afraid. Unlike the bodies that he had cut into before then, these ones cried out in response to his lack of surgical proficiency. Where he had previously anxiously anticipated people's deaths, now Vesalius was responsible for their lives.

Following the campaign for Guelders, when the winter rest began to set in, Vesalius returned anxiously to his home university of Padua only to find that his student, Colombo, who held the anatomy chair named after Vesalius, had been undermining his master's expertise and taking credit for discoveries he had not made. Vesalius was hurt and disgusted by Colombo's disloyalty, but he nonetheless remained open to the warm reception he received from others at Padua. This would not be his experience in Bologna, for despite the enthusiasm of the students and faculty, Vesalius knew that his words and demonstration had been met with deaf ears and blind eyes. When he finally arrived in Pisa, Vesalius was not simply welcomed but was treated with sincere reverence. How Vesalius must have needed this recognition after being alienated from his true passion while at war! Is it not possible that, upon returning from battle, Vesalius recognized that he was best suited to academic life and did not want to follow in his family's footsteps?

Frustrated that his home, medicine, was also home to many disloyal, ignorant, and self-serving inhabitants, Vesalius may have felt weakened in confidence upon returning from the battlefields and susceptible to the baseless attacks from his critics. However, when on the verge of returning to a life of service he did not want, Vesalius must have seen Pisa as a place where he could return to his work and fulfill the greater destiny he sensed was within him. Thus, it may in fact have been Vesalius who encouraged the duke to write to the emperor on his behalf and ask for his release. Vesalius, who had before the *Fabrica*'s release and its dedication to the emperor, been completely free to choose his future path, had found himself locked into the very position he had previously aspired to obtain.

Sylvius would come to call Vesalius a madman because he would not conform to accepted traditional ways of thinking; but in conforming to familial and personal expectation, Vesalius did truly go mad. When the emperor refused to release him from service, Vesalius experienced the full trauma of an identity crisis. Unable to cope with the reality of receiving exactly what he had asked for, imperial service, and unable to comprehend that he had to leave behind not only his academic life but also his own awaiting potential, Vesalius was overcome with madness and grief, causing him to throw his precious notes, laboured drawings, and treasured books into the fire. Understanding fully that his life was longer his own, but someone else's, Vesalius surrendered that part of himself that he most identified with, and effectively killed it. By burning his work, Vesalius destroyed his identity as a scholar and as an anatomist, and assuming the role of tragic hero, was forced to reconcile with the impossible reality that he had turned away from his own destiny.

But just as the tragic hero does not understand that his failure and profound disappointment have already been taken into account by destiny, Vesalius did not realize where his real potential lay. In the first unexpected turn in Vesalius's story, he was forced to leave Paris and return to Louvain. Just as that event became the unexpected means by which he came to pursue the art of dissection, his being forced to assume the position of a regular physician would result in Vesalius reaching far beyond the destiny that he had imagined for himself.

SECTION THREE: THE MYTH

The voyage of discovery is not in seeking new landscapes, but in having new eyes.

—Marcel Proust

Throughout his education and professional life, Vesalius's expressed desire was to unite the study of medicine with its practice. However, it would not be until his experience as a military field surgeon that he would substantively understand the significance of this aspiration.

No longer resentful of his imperial sentence, Vesalius came to recognize that his comprehensive studies of anatomy and the human body were in fact the necessary prerequisites for a conscientious and effective practice in therapeutic medicine. As Vesalius slowly began to reintroduce himself into academic circles, it became clear that a new project was developing within his mind's eye: a new comprehensive model of medical practice that would dwarf his past achievements. Unfortunately, by the cruelty of the fates, he would never have the chance to share it.

CHAPTER EIGHT

Anatomist Turned Physician

IN THE LATE SPRING OR early summer of 1544, after nearly six months of traveling and performing anatomy demonstrations at universities throughout northern Italy, Vesalius traveled from Florence to rejoin the emperor and his entourage. Though battles had ceased for the winter, diplomatic quarrels between the king of France, Francis I, and Holy Roman Emperor Charles V continued in Ghent and Brussels. As Charles endured yet another bout of gout, he continued planning for the next phase of war and the Diet (a regular meeting of the German estates) which was set to open in early winter in Speyer along the Rhine in southwest Germany. The emperor was faced with serious political problems within the summit; for, in addition to dealing with the ongoing conflicts between the Lutheran and Catholic princes and with the growing movement within the German estates to seek greater independence, Charles was determined to secure more men and material support for his war with France. The presence of Pope Paul III, in the form of his representative, Alessandro Farnese, complicated matters at the Diet still further by interrupting the emperor's sovereign capacity to direct the meeting's discourse and priorities.

Vesalius joined the emperor in Speyer and was working again as a military surgeon by early July during the siege of Saint Dizier. Vesalius's return marked the formal start of his imperial service; and he was henceforth fully commissioned as a regular household physician for the next thirteen years. Vesalius's career and his personal life became governed, not by academic debate and formal study, but by the whims and concerns of his employer, the emperor. Despite these limits on his day-to-day intellectual freedoms, Vesalius would, through his imperial service, come to advance his own applied knowledge of medicine to such a degree that his findings would break new ground within the discipline of clinical medicine itself and allow him to tap into a potential that would have otherwise remained dormant.

i. The Spoils of War

In mid-July, Vesalius examined the body of one of the emperor's most promising young commanders, René, Prince of Orange, who was fatally wounded in the arm by cannon fire. As part of his wartime duties, Vesalius was responsible for preparing and embalming the bodies of deceased noblemen so that they could be transported to their homelands for burial. These procedures provided Vesalius with some opportunity to make detailed anatomical observations, though the demands of the work made such studies hasty and incomplete. In caring for the wounded, Vesalius also learned to adapt his dissection skills to the exercise of surgery and amputation, an unpleasant and excruciating education.

Although the Spanish had a reputation for being conservative and conventional to a fault in their understanding of medicine, Vesalius and the surgeon Daza Chacon had developed an open and strong professional relationship, and while working in the field together, they developed new surgical techniques and treatments. For instance, during the siege of Saint Dizier, Vesalius and Chacon adopted a less traumatic and more efficacious method of treating gunshot wounds. Rather than cauterizing wounds or applying hot oil, they used cleansing and soothing unguents to ward off infection, an advancement that benefited both patient and physician. (Although two well-known physicians, Maggi and LaGuna, are credited with pioneering this practice, their findings had yet to be widely recognized during this time.) In the urgency of field medicine, the evidence obtained through observation was by far the most convincing teacher of therapeutic treatment. Unfortunately, however, the invisible spread of infection (through the use of dirty cloths and unsterile instruments) appeared to the pre-germ-theory, sixteenth-century physician to be spontaneous occurrences inherent to patients' injuries or illnesses and unrelated to the method of their treatment.

As his second season of war came to an end, Vesalius found that he had become far advanced in his clinical skills and had developed expertise both as a military surgeon and as a medical practitioner. Charles V and Francis I agreed in September of 1544 to terms of peace in the Treaty of Crépy. The agreement would be broken in less than a year after the death of Francis's son, the Duke of Orléans, whose future marriage to a relative of Charles V was the basis upon which the treaty was signed; but the talks, which were held in Brussels, reunited Vesalius with his family and friends and presented the opportunity for him to marry. Just shy of his thirtieth birthday, in November of 1544, Vesalius wed Anne van Hamme, the daughter of a Brussels city councilor and master of the Chamber of Accounts. The extreme cold of the winter aggravated the emperor's gout to such an extent that he was prevented from traveling to Worms for the year's German Diet. It seems that Vesalius and his new wife were happy for this prolonged stay, for late the following summer, Vesalius and his wife welcomed the birth of a little girl, Anne. Just as his father had been, Vesalius was attending to his imperial duties in Germany at the time of his child's birth.

ii. Imperial Reality

For the first two years of service to the emperor, Vesalius acted as a military surgeon, but in the spring of 1545, he was called to the emperor's side. Charles V had an enormous imperial court that numbered in the hundreds. The emperor was an enthusiast of alternative medicine, and his medical advisors included numerous empiric healers who addressed his multiple ailments by creative and unconventional means. With such a diverse demographic among court members, Vesalius was surprised when his introduction was met with disdain and hostility by a group of court physicians, most of whom were Spanish. Having studied at

Louvain, Paris, and Padua, Vesalius had been exposed to and worked intimately with an international community of scholars, intellectuals, and professionals; but never before had he experienced such deliberate intimidation and unsubstantiated criticism. Vesalius later characterized these detractors as "the unlearned who disregard all study and think only of making money."[228] As he would later write in his *Letter on the China Root*, the obtuseness of his critics and their unrelenting commitment to theories empirically proven to be wrong frustrated him to no end. As the most educated and talented member of the emperor's team of physicians, Vesalius eventually came to be held in the highest esteem by the majority of the courtiers and citizenry and revered for his practice by the emperor himself. However, in 1545, in the first years following the release of the *Fabrica*, Vesalius found himself repeatedly forced to defend his work and his reputation among his colleagues.

In addition to adapting to the conditions of the emperor's court, Vesalius was also beginning to understand the burden of being in personal service to a stubborn patient prone to chronic medical conditions, many of which were caused and exacerbated by the patient's habits of great excess. From his youth, Charles of Ghent had not been an easy or cooperative patient. Among his more serious concerns, Charles had suffered from asthma and other respiratory illnesses throughout his childhood. As heir to the Burgundian Empire, Charles grew up with rich traditions, ceremonies, and lavish feasts. So receptive was he of the gratuities of his position that by the age of thirty, the health of this gourmand began to suffer. In 1528, Charles had his first attack of gout, known as "rich man's disease." A form of arthritis, gout is characterized by pain and swelling in the joints caused by the body's inability to properly rid itself of excess uric acid. Certain foods rich in the chemical purine encourage uric acid production. Charles's steady and abundant diet of game and rich organ meats such as kidney, liver, and heart; his love for small vats of sardines and anchovies, beer and alcohol; and his increasingly sedentary life forced his physicians to regularly prescribe a treatment regimen consisting of dietary changes, moderate exercise, and an array of pharmaceutical concoctions with which his advisors experimented. Despite brief periods of compliance and improvement, Charles regularly refused the advice of council and remained unchanged in his appetites. For example, the emperor's daily schedule was as follows: Upon arising at five, he had a "light" breakfast of a draught of beer and a stewed fowl, followed by a nap. Later he arose to attend a private mass, greet scheduled audiences, and attend public mass. This was followed by a big midday meal consisting of as many as twenty dishes of mostly meat and fish. Later in the evening, Charles typically enjoyed a large dish of anchovies and a midnight supper with more rich foods. Though he drank moderately for the times, wine or beer accompanied all of his meals.[229] With the emperor's great propensity for gluttony, there was little that Charles's team of physicians could do to improve his health. At best, they worked to alleviate his most uncomfortable symptoms.

Like many who suffer from chronic conditions, the emperor was constantly on the hunt for a cure and often too ready to embrace the latest miracle treatment. At the time of Vesalius's arrival, the emperor's gout was primarily treated with a decoction derived from "China root," the efficacy of which was suspect to Vesalius. Although he was not Charles's primary physician—and thus was relieved of many dealings with his unsophisticated patient—part of Vesalius's duties for years to come would entail assisting in managing the health of one whose life was of great import to many. As Charles's confessor advised him in 1530, "Remember that your life is not your own but should be preserved for the sake of others, and if your Majesty chooses to destroy your own property, you should not endanger what belongs to us."[230] Despite such wisdom, there appears to be no evidence to suggest that appeals to the emperor's conscience, such as this, were any more effective than those directed to his reason by his physicians.

iii. The "Letter" on the China Root

Sometime within the first year of Vesalius's formal service, the emperor called upon Gerard van Veltwyck, a learned botanist and friend of Vesalius's from Louvain, to act as a diplomatic representative on a mission to the Ottoman court in Turkey. Given a brief opportunity to visit, Vesalius inquired at great length about Veltwyck's latest discoveries and questioned him on his knowledge of Charles's favored gout treatment, the Turkish China root. Shortly following their visit, on June 13, 1546, Vesalius wrote a letter in response to a request posed by his friend, Joachim Roelants, a physician from Mechelen. Roelant had asked Vesalius to:

> describe the way in which the decoction of the so-called
> china root was recently given to the emperor and to many
> others of our court, as well as [Vesalius's] opinion about
> the results obtained and for what diseases it was used.[231]

Vesalius's response would be his first effort to position himself once again within academic circles.

In addressing the China root, Vesalius informs his audience that many German physicians have been anxious to know the precise method by which he used the medicament in the treatment of the emperor, so that they too could soundly recommend it to their own imperial patients. It seems Vesalius included this peripheral piece of information as a way of informing his audience that other royal physicians turned to him for advice and that he remained, as he was, an authority in his field, despite his change in position.

It is clear from early in his address that Vesalius wished to distance himself from the herbal medicine in question, by suggesting that it was through its use by the Emperor, not its effectiveness, that the China root had become a popular medicine: "Such is the popularity the emperor's name has given this medicine in a brief time, although in fact he has taken it more by his own choice than on the advice of Master Cornelius." The first half of the letter is devoted to an examination of the drug from which he had concluded that: first, there was little information about its origin or its history; and second, there was no definitive evidence to support the drug's efficacy. Vesalius nonetheless concedes that the emperor's recent haphazard use of the China root left him in better health than he had been in the previous year.

Vesalius recounts within the letter the event of his burning his books, writings, and drawing and addresses his resentment of the critical atmosphere surrounding his research findings, particularly those assaults from Sylvius. Here, once again, we see Vesalius shrewdly adopting the self-effacing form of a personal correspondence (epistola) to present his scholarly insights and respond to his most vocal critics. Although Vesalius most surely expected that his words would eventually reach a public audience, his critical and defensive discussion nonetheless remains veiled in the humble appearance of a private letter in response to a friend's pressing question, a gesture which gives his words an air of authenticity and modesty. The second half of the letter steers away from analysis of the drug and is substantively devoted to a defense against Sylvius's virulent attacks on Vesalius and his *Fabrica*.

Upon receiving the letter, Roelants allowed Vesalius's brother, Franciscus Vesalius, to take the liberty of copying the letter by hand. This rendition was then sent to Joannes Oporinus who published it later that year, 1546, as *Epistola on the China Root*. The letter was already circulating widely before its publication, but Oporinus reasoned that if he did not, some other printer whose motivation was driven by profit, not product, would publish it instead. Needless to say, the manuscript was a success, not only for its information on the China root, which was the stated purpose, but also because it secured Vesalius's continued participation within scholarly circles and allowed him to defend himself despite being absent from direct debate.

CHAPTER NINE

The Art of Diagnosis

BETWEEN 1546 AND 1548, VESALIUS began his own court practice as he traveled through Germany with Charles V, who was then attempting to squash a rebellion of Protestant princes who had banded together into a loose confederation known as the Schmalkaldic League. Although many Catholics of Northern Europe, including Charles, felt that the Church needed some reform, he rejected the Lutheran and Protestant positions as heretical. Charles V was a devout Catholic who genuinely perceived his overarching task as emperor to be to defend Christendom and promote the unity of the Church of Rome. But as a titular ruler of the German Estates, his power came from persuasion, diplomacy, and bribery—not position. Religious conflict, combined with the intermittent warring with the French and the Turkish encroachment on Europe, meant that Charles remained in residence in northern Europe. This generally provided Vesalius with enough stability to develop his own practice. Throughout his education and professional life, Vesalius expressed a desire to unite the study and practice of medicine. The therapeutic arts, he believed, had been:

> ravaged by having its primary instrument, the application of the hand's work in healing, so neglected that it seemed to have been handed over to common folk and to persons completely untrained in the disciplines that serve the medical art.[232]

In other words, those who were in the practice of medicine knew little of anatomical theory and scholarship, and those who studied medical philosophy had been completely separated from the practice of pharmacology and surgery. Vesalius wished to emulate the ancient Greeks, as he understood them, and restore this unity within his own practice. In doing so, Vesalius saw his comprehensive studies of the anatomy of the human body as the prerequisite knowledge for the conscientious and effective practice of therapeutic medicine. Developing a contribution to medicine along this vein could have theoretically forwarded the medical arts of the sixteenth century into previously unimagined levels of efficacy.

i. A Man of Mythic Proportions

From as early as 1545, Vesalius's reputation as a capable clinical physician and talented surgeon had burgeoned. Called upon to treat a prominent Flemish knight and personal attendant of the emperor, he and Daza Chacon sought to resolve the mystery of his injury. For as long as three months, the man had suffered from a pain in his inner right thigh that was so severe that he could not eat or sleep. The conventional treatments of bleeding, purging, and medicaments had proven ineffective. As Chacon recorded:

> We went to him to open the place where the pain was located, although there was no sign of any obstruction, and drew off a quantity of slightly whitish matter. As it came forth, instantly the sick man commenced to rest, to eat, and to sleep; and the outcome was so successful that where he had been almost consumed, now in a short time—as he was a youth—he was restored to full health.[233]

This case is largely quoted as being the *first* use of surgery to treat chronic osteomyelitis, a secondary bacterial infection of the bone and bone marrow. This would not be the only vanguard treatment that Vesalius would help to develop.

In 1547, Daza Chacon recorded Vesalius's use of surgery to attempt to open and drain a collection of pus, called *empyema*, from the pleural cavity, a surgical treatment that Vesalius had drawn from Hippocratic texts. Although Vesalius's instincts were good, the surgical lancing of the suspected infection produced no drainage, and the patient died. But by the early 1560s, Vesalius was reporting many successful cases of surgically treating *empyema*. This technique proved very useful in an era when warfare and tournament combat commonly produced penetrating chest and thoracic wounds that resulted in infection and fistulas that would not heal. Vesalius's success led to greater acceptance of this useful technique, and today a form of the practice remains, which entails inserting a chest tube to drain the pus.

In December of 1548, at the end of his first five years as imperial physician, one correct diagnosis elevated Vesalius's reputation to something close to legend. Maximilian of Egmont, the Count of Buren and a Knight of the Golden Fleece, fell severely ill upon returning to Brussels following a diplomatic mission to England. Vesalius went to him immediately. After examining the count, Vesalius told him quietly and directly that he believed the ill man had only five to six hours to live. As a good friend, he wisely advised Buren to look after his affairs. The count took the news calmly and called to his side his two closest companions, Anthony de Perrenot (the bishop of Arras) and the Count of Aremberg. Supported by these friends, he made his will, offered his last confession, and received the Holy Sacrament. With these private matters accomplished, the count rose and dressed in his finest, richest clothing, donned his best armor, and had the collar and cloak of the Order of the Golden Fleece placed around his neck and shoulders. Lastly, he placed his favorite hat, made in the Polish style, upon his head and took up his sword.

Brilliantly dressed and armed, he carried himself into his reception hall where many of his captains and officers had gathered to pay their final respects. Looking around to those gathered, Egmont commended them all to God before taking each one and offering recompense "according to their merits, giving a horse to this one, a mule to that, and to another a greyhound or a complete set of clothing."[234] The count then asked for some wine that he might drink to his imperial lord's health. When the drink arrived, he offered a brief but affecting account of his life and the honors bestowed upon him by his royal master; then he removed the collar of the Golden Fleece and handed it to his dear friend the Count of Aremberg. With great effort, Egmont rose and drank to his majesty. Sensing the end was near, he commended his dear friends the bishop and the count to God, and then embraced his attending physician, Andreas Vesalius, "thanking him for his timely warning." With "a noble and unsurpassed courage," Egmont asked to be taken to his bed, and then he died. In performing the postmortem, Vesalius found an advanced, pus-ridden abscess in the upper thorax in the cavity between the lungs. As a commander and personage, the Count of Buren had been much admired for his character and integrity, and his ceremonious death so moved observers "that a whole generation of literature, sentimental and heroic sprang from the event."[235] Vesalius would be forever immortalized as the man who, with divine-like insight, allowed the noblest of men to remain so even in his death.

It has also been suggested that Vesalius was the first modern physician to recognize and describe an internal aneurysm in a living person. Called to Augsberg by his physician friends, Vesalius examined a member of the famous Welser banking family.[236] Master Welser had begun to experience continuous and severe pain after a horseback ride, though he had not been injured or in an accident. Finding a pulsating mass on Welser's back near the vertebrae, Vesalius diagnosed an aortic aneurysm, which he determined could prove fatal at any time. The patient lived for another two years but remained in constant anguish. After the man's death, an autopsy performed by one of the attending physicians, Vesalius's friend Achilles Gasser, confirmed the original diagnosis. Gasser wrote to Vesalius to describe how the enlargement had ballooned to such a degree that the expanded walls of the aorta had adhered to the ribs and vertebrae. Vesalius responded that he also had observed several extreme aneurysms in various parts of patients' bodies, including one in the sister of their mutual friend, Anthony Perrenot de Granvelle. Her aneurysm could be felt in the abdomen below the stomach and was "so loose that you might consider it to be a ball which, as she lies on this side or that, is driven now to the left, now to the right."[237] Remarkably, she lived with the palpable aneurysm for some years. The occurrence of such obviously discernible cases led Vesalius to speculate to his colleague, "If we frequently discover [an aneurysm] lying concealed in the body of the living, how often may it be hidden from us in the brain, in the thoracic cavity, and around the pelvic region."[238] Vesalius's conjecture has been confirmed by modern diagnostic imaging, which has found, for example, the existence of cerebral aneurysms that cause strokes when ruptured.

Vesalius had become invaluable to the court. When the Venetian ambassador fell seriously ill with a fever, the Venetians expressed great gratitude to the emperor for having such a distinguished physician as Vesalius stay behind to provide for his care. Other high-ranking members of the court also sought and favored his advice, and although Vesalius formally ranked behind Baersdorp in caring for Charles V, various reports suggest that the emperor secretly preferred Vesalius's care. In addition to his personal treatment, Vesalius was also frequently solicited to perform diagnostics at a distance when baffled physicians wrote to him with details of their patients' puzzling ailments. In the surviving medical records (*concilia*) that Vesalius kept, it appears that he typically expressed reservations about coming to definitive conclusions and diagnoses without first examining the patient himself. For example, in his 1547 reply to Bathasar von Stubenberg, Vesalius discusses the case of a boy whose foot was so drawn that he walked only on the side of it.

> The more I examine and consider the report sent to me, the less I know what to write, for in order that ailments be properly understood not little description is required, as well as careful and frequent examination together with the correct medicine; these things provide a considerable part of the knowledge of such ailments.[239]

The import that Vesalius accorded to firsthand empirical observation had been the foundation of his practice since he first began to "study the bones." But unlike in his academic life, Vesalius's insights as a physician were welcomed. Where Vesalius was before subject to fruitless debates over which writer of antiquity was more "true," the practical life of a surgeon allowed him to draw from his scholarship and apply it to therapeutic practice. Despite having dismissed any hope for a meaningful and challenging future, Vesalius found in his position under Emperor Charles V a tremendous opportunity and freedom to study, to reflect, and to practice all that he had learned.

> We are constantly faced with burdens which make us wish for escape from this life, as all those know who take pleasure in publishing the results of their researches—men who, because they do not know how to be born and pass away unnoticed, so expose themselves to all sorts of insults. It is their own fault that they constantly hear remarks about their writings that gnaw at the soul, and it is for that reason that I am content to live at court far from the sweet leisure of studies.[240]

Anatomical research remained an integral part of Vesalius's work, and he allowed no opportunity for analysis to be overlooked. One of the most unusual opportunities that Vesalius took to study anatomical differences came on May 18, 1552, when Maurice of Saxony marched on Innsbruck, forcing the emperor and a small entourage, including Vesalius, to flee under the cover of night by a treacherous mountain pass (the Brenner Pass) before continuing east to safety in Austria and the traditional Habsburg strongholds. In Vesalius's reserved account of the perilous journey, he suggests that the experience, though harrowing, gave him the rare opportunity to compare the anatomical features of peoples from different communities.

> We set forth from Innsbruck in the greatest haste for Villach, where I was astonished to see how different from my previous observations were the skulls in the cemeteries of Styria and Carinthia—which produce different and strange types of men both in mind and in body, thereby demonstrating nature's many whims as regards shape.[241]

ii. Out with the Old, In with the New

Vesalius's extensive responsibilities to the emperor and to his practice necessarily did not provide ample opportunity for dissection and anatomical analysis; however, traveling throughout Germany as a member of the emperor's entourage did provide Vesalius with the welcomed opportunity to interact with other physicians who shared an interest in anatomical research. Through the kindness of physicians who resided in cities like Augsburg, where the emperor and his court had temporarily settled, Vesalius found friendship among like-minded physicians who provided him with ample opportunities for dissection. This productive period of research allowed Vesalius to bring to print a new edition of the *Fabrica* in 1555.

While using the same woodblocks from the 1543 edition, Vesalius made numerous revisions and corrections; and he detailed extensive new observations gathered while working in the company of the German physicians. In the additions to the 1555 edition, Vesalius introduced various anatomical anomalies that he had observed in his medical practice and through autopsy. Among the cases described were the abnormalities caused by an ovarian cyst in the uterus and ovaries of a fifty-year-old woman, the grossly distorted heart of a man who had possibly suffered a partial heart aneurysm, and the distorted parts of the brain caused by hydrocephaly in a two-year-old girl. Perhaps because the original, unprecedented, cross-disciplined impact of the *Fabrica* in 1543 had less to do with the details of its content than with the introduction of anatomical illustration derived from dissection; or perhaps because Vesalius no longer moved within the academic community of northern Europe, and the energy and controversy surrounding his work and character, which had helped to bolster the success of the first edition, was noticeably absent from the release of the second edition; or perhaps because Vesalius had been so successful in moving anatomical research toward empirical rather traditional study that it was impossible to create the same impact in the field of medicine as was felt in 1543—whatever the reason—the release of the 1555 edition of Vesalius's *Fabrica* did not receive much attention until the early 1900s.

In retrospect, the significance of the text was again, not in the details of its content, but in Vesalius's attempt to contribute to medical scholarship and practice by introducing a work that seamlessly married his previous anatomical study with findings derived form clinical practice.

As the emperor's health problems persisted, it became apparent that he would soon abdicate his titles and present his son, Philip II of Spain, with the Spanish empire of which he was already regent. Vesalius may have timed the publication of the new edition out of gratitude to the emperor for the freedom and opportunity to expand his clinical expertise that his years of imperial service had accorded him. Vesalius may have also considered returning to a university position after Charles's abdication and could have wanted to reintroduce himself to academic circles. In 1556, the Holy Roman Emperor Charles V stepped down from his position, and on September 21, 1558, he died.

Before Philip II received the Spanish Crown, Vesalius received from Charles V a pension for life and was made Count Palatine. It is not known whether Vesalius remained in service to Philip because he was satisfied with the new monarch or because leaving the service was not an option, but the decision to remain would indirectly prove a to be a fatal one.

iii. Death of a King

After King Henri II of France concluded the April 1559 Peace Treaty of Cateau-Cambresis with his longtime enemies, the Habsburgs of Austria, he immediately returned to Paris to begin preparations for an elaborate festival that would mark the June marriage of his daughter Elizabeth of Valois to King Philip II of Spain. In addition to the planned feasts, the celebration would be punctuated with a three-day tournament. King Philip II cared nothing for such ceremonies, nor was he interested in the girl he was to marry. "Kings of Spain," he said, "do not go after their brides." Thus Philip sent the Duke of Alba from Brussels to stand in for him and wed by proxy the thirteen-year-old Elizabeth.

On the last day of the tournament, June 30, King Henri was strongly advised not to participate in the day's jousting. But the French king was an avid fan of such events and entered himself to run several courses that day. After the third course, the king appeared overheated and tired but, feeling that he had performed poorly in the last pass, demanded another course. In readying for the run, the king unwisely left his helmet visor unsecured. Whether the visor was left up intentionally or because the latch had been weakened by earlier blows, the conditions were set for an unforeseen tragedy.

In jousting, the lances are not held by the arm on the side closest to the opponent, but are held across the body by the opposite outside arm. On the king's final run, the lance of Gabriel Montgomery, captain of the king's Scottish Guard, was, according to Vesalius,

> broken through its neck by the impact in such a way that, on strike that part of the helmet below the eyes, the end of the splintered lance, still held in the hand of the noble, drove upward as if by a second thrust into the face of the king, at that time unprotected.[242]

The blow first struck the king across the eyebrows and bridge of the nose and then continued across to the right temple. At the same time, splinters from the lance were thrust between the eyeball and its socket, causing trauma to the brain. The king somehow managed to remain in his saddle and dismount, but shortly after lost consciousness. He then recovered enough to climb the stairs to his bedchamber without assistance.

The court physicians and surgeons, including Ambrose Paré (thought by many to be the most renowned and innovative surgeon of the sixteenth century), rushed to attend to the king. The most accessible splinters were extracted and his wounds dressed. The king was then given a purgative and moderately bled. As the king received treatment, the Duke of Savoy sent an urgent message by rider to Brussels to request from King Philip the aid of Vesalius. Receiving the message on July 2, Philip sent Vesalius off in great haste.

Arriving on July 3, Vesalius found that in the four days since the injury, the King Henri had not improved. Additional splinters had been removed as they expressed themselves from the wound, but the king remained in a befuddled sleep despite having only a slight fever. Although the king's skull did not appear to be fractured, many of the physicians feared an injury to the brain. Upon arriving and examining the patient, Vesalius performed a simple diagnostic test: Placing a clean white cloth between the king's teeth, Vesalius asked him to bite down upon it. When the king complied, Vesalius pulled the cloth out quickly and forcefully. The king cried out in pain, clapping his hand to his head. This result clearly signified to Vesalius that the wound would not heal and that the king's condition would continue to deteriorate until his death. Six days later, on July 10, King Henri II of France succumbed to his injuries. Vesalius and Paré both helped to perform Henri's autopsy, and each concluded in his own account that the head injuries sustained by the king were evidence of the fact that serious brain injury could occur even in the absence of a fractured skull, a new observation of the mid-sixteenth century.

Shortly after his return from Paris, Vesalius and his family sailed with King Philip's entourage to take up a new position with the king in Spain. Up until this point, Vesalius had been able to continue his anatomical investigations as part of his practical medical duties within the court; however, in the conservative and pious climate of Spain, Vesalius would find a community most hostile towards his practice, research, and person.

iv. The Telltale Spanish Heart

In 1559, the Spanish kingdoms of King Philip II were neither progressive in their practices nor receptive to reformative scholarship. Among all of the Catholic European states, the Spanish realms of Castile and Aragon were the most dogmatic and militantly orthodox. The Spanish monarchs of the late fifteenth century worked to drive out the last of the Moors from the Iberian Peninsula—in the name of the Church—and forced the Jewish community to convert to Catholicism or face expulsion. In recognition of their success and commitment, the pope bestowed upon Philip II's great-grandparents, King Ferdinand and Queen Isabella, the title of Catholic Majesties. Although the Spanish Inquisition had been founded in 1480 to ensure that converted Jews remained loyal to their new faith, by the late sixteenth century, the Inquisition had grown into a blanket defense against all forms of dissidence, fueled by the appearance of the Protestant movement that had divided Germany and had begun threatening the Netherlands and France.

Throughout his reign, Charles V relied heavily on Spain to provide troops and finances to support his military efforts in defending Christendom and the Church from attacks by Protestant reformers. Thus, when Phillip II was crowned the king of Spain in 1556, the country's sense of self-importance became manifest in the belief that Spain had become a major power. This pride, however, did not reflect reality. Spanish society remained decidedly insular in its cultural, social, and political views and thus presented only a marginal influence on the rest of Europe. The Spanish were, in effect, stuck in an allegiance with the past. In terms of medical discourse, while the rest of Europe was shaking off the husks of medieval thought, Spanish scholars of the sixteenth century, despite having once been leaders of scholarship and education, continued to adhere strictly to Galenic medical theory as it had been interpreted by the Arabic and Jewish traditions. For example, learned medicine was gradually moving away from its heavy reliance on astrology; however, the Spanish Cortes (Castile's representative assembly) continued to urge Philip II to create astrological chairs in medicine at the Spanish universities so that medical students could learn "to relate the movements of planets with the critical days of illness."[243]

Although he had been born, raised, and educated in Castile, Philip II shared his father's love of learning and believed in expanding the breadth of Spanish education so long as it was consistent with the Catholic orthodoxy "imposed largely by Thomism and enforced by the Inquisition."[244] While Philip's outlook was more open than that of many of his subjects, he nonetheless remained fearful that infidels would infiltrate his country and corrupt his beloved people. In 1559, King Philip II issued an edict forbidding Spanish students from studying in universities outside of Spanish territories, unless they sought an education from the Catholic centers of Rome, Naples, or Bologna. So archaic and backwards were Spanish medical thought and practice that one Tuscan ambassador commented, "Who hasn't seen it can't believe it."[245] Having forbade the practice of dissection, Spanish medicine remained in a world where the body was either approached through the lenses of antiquity or astrology, or remained an object of complete mystery.

As mentioned above, it is not clear why Vesalius accepted service under King Philip II. Numerous accounts suggest that Philip preferred to surround himself with Spanish advisors and courtiers and often exhibited a lack of ease when dealing with individuals from different backgrounds. The Venetian ambassador, Suriano, stated that Philip was "disliked by Italians, disagreeable to Flemings, and hateful to Germans."[246] Despite this, all evidence suggests that Philip II genuinely held Vesalius in the highest esteem for his medical knowledge and clinical skills, and thus likely wished to keep this valued resource at his side for his own safety and that of the son that he hoped Elizabeth would bear. What makes Vesalius's relationship with Philip all the more puzzling was that Vesalius accepted, under the new king, a far less prestigious position within the royal court than he had held under Charles V. Instead of assuming the role of personal physician to the king or household, Vesalius was named a "court physician" to the Netherlanders and was responsible for attending to the German states and most foreign ambassadors and dignitaries. This was no doubt a political move on Philip II's part, for it would likely have been impossible for a Flemish physician, regardless of experience and reputation, to hold the position of "personal assistant" within the Spanish court. Additionally, situating Vesalius in his new position was a strong diplomatic move on Phillip's part since, unlike the king, Vesalius was well-respected in foreign circles and could thus act as an informal mediator in his diplomatic relations. That Vesalius and Phillip had come to a kind of working agreement in relation to his position must be assumed, but the details of that relationship remain unknown.

In Gabriel Fallopio's 1561 publication, *Observationes anatomicae* (*Anatomical Observations*), the "spiritual disciple" of Vesalius used the findings of the *Fabrica* to anchor his own journey of anatomical study. Inspired and uplifted by Fallopio's accolades and reverent analysis, Vesalius was forced to reflect upon his academic aspirations and the limits set upon him in his marginal medical position under Phillip II. On May

2, 1564, Vesalius published a thoughtful response to Fallopio's work, entitled *Anatomicarum Gabrielis Falopii Observationum Examen Augustinus Gadaldinus*. Follopino.

At the time that Vesalius wrote his essay, Fallopio was employed by the University of Padua and held Vesalius's chair in the instruction of anatomy. It was also well known that he was in very poor health. Considering these details, particular aspects of Vesalius's publication and its possible implications position the *Examen* as a bold and strategic gesture as evidenced by the following: first, the nature of Vesalius's retort to Fallopio's critique completely contradicted the sacrosanct adherence to Galen common among Spanish physicians; and second, Vesalius indicates a readiness to return to academic scholarship. Since Vesalius was masterful at weaving subtle debates and had expressed private desires within many of his published essays and correspondences, it is reasonable to suggest that the essential, though tacit, intention of the *Examen*'s publication was to sow the seeds of his release from imperial position and facilitate his return to Padua. By taking a position at such odds with Galenic ideology, Vesalius undoubtedly and predictably incited aggression towards him by his fellow Spanish physicians. This kind of unrest within his court could compel Phillip II to release Vesalius from service and leave him free—for the first time in nearly two decades—to return to the university.

Additionally, by responding to Fallopio, Vesalius not only made it clear that he remained intellectually attuned and advanced in his following of the relevant discourse of the day, but he also drew the attention of the University of Padua, which was presumably looking to find a successor for the ailing Fallopio. Understood in this way, the *Examen* appears to be, not a formal essay, per se, but rather an elaborate job application.

Whatever Vesalius's intention, two things are known: first, Vesalius left Spain in 1564 under unknown conditions to make a pilgrimage to Jerusalem; and two, the *Examen* was the last work that Vesalius ever published.

The first account of the events leading up to Vesalius's departure from Spain appears in a 1620 biography on Vesalius. In it, the author includes a letter apparently written in Paris in 1565 by a diplomat named Hubert

Languet. It is not known how Languet came by the letter or the story. According to this account from an unknown source, Vesalius left Spain to undertake a pilgrimage to Jerusalem because he had performed an autopsy on a patient who turned out to be still alive.

> A Spanish nobleman had been entrusted to his care, but when Vesalius believed him to have died, and because he was not satisfied as to the cause of his death, he sought permission from the relatives of the dead man to open the body; having obtained such permission, when he opened the chest he found the heart still beating. The relatives, not content to accuse Vesalius of murder, also denounced him before the Inquisition as impious, thus seeking to gain an even greater revenge. When the cause of death was explained, it was not easy to excuse such error on the part of so skilled a physician, and the Inquisition fully determined upon his execution. It was only with the greatest difficulty that the king by his authority, or rather his supplication, was able to save him. The prayers of king and court were finally heeded on condition that Vesalius expiate his crime by a journey to Jerusalem and Mount Sinai.[247]

A 1571 account by Ambrose Paré offered a corroborating account of an unintentional postmortem on a woman who was presumed dead but then proved to still be alive. Paré does not name the physician involved, but some later writers assumed it was Vesalius, based on Paré's description of the erring physician as "un grand anatomiste, je dis grand et celebre" and "a great anatomist, great and celebrated,"[248] Like Languet's version, Pare's account was also from an unverifiable source.

Modern biographers of Vesalius reject the credibility of these reports. After nearly five hundred years of interest and research on Vesalius, there is no further evidence that this scandalous occurrence ever took place: No evidence has been found in the records of the Inquisition; no public or political record mentions these charges; and the letter attributed to

Languet was not included in his published letters and, by all accounts, has never been found. This is not to say that the accusations had not been made against Vesalius, for other famous anatomists, including Berengario da Carpi and Fallopio, had also been falsely accused of similar gross errors. Even without considering the question of whether so skilled a physician as Vesalius could have erred so egregiously, the story remains unsubstantiated and thus highly suspect. There is no surviving original correspondence detailing the occurrence, and the only account remaining is from a second-hand source appearing almost sixty years after Vesalius's death.

Another theory as to why Vesalius left Spain for Jerusalem suggests that he genuinely desired to make the pilgrimage. In one of the most credible accounts, Charles de l'Ecluse claims to have been a close witness to Vesalius's departure. Although he arrived in Madrid just shortly after Vesalius took leave, l'Ecluse received information on Vesalius's whereabouts from a man who was well acquainted with him, Charles de Tisnacq, a counselor to the Netherlanders in court. According to this account, Vesalius had suffered a severe illness, from which recovery was difficult and slow; and he had vowed to make a pilgrimage to Jerusalem out of gratitude should he recover. Modern biographers question the authenticity of Vesalius's long ailment since he had been active in his practice late in January and left for his journey in March. Vesalius's biographer, C. D. O'Malley, speculates that Vesalius, in a ploy to leave Spain, represented his minor illness as a grave sickness and under that pretense implored the king to allow him to make a pilgrimage to the Holy Land.[249] This too cannot be confirmed.

Whatever the truth is behind Vesalius's departure, it is known that he and his wife and daughter left Madrid by coach in March of 1564, with a letter of safe passage from the king in hand. Although this letter was intended to guarantee that he and his family would pass smoothly through various customs offices, Vesalius reportedly created a scene with custom officials at the first outpost he encountered on the border town of Perpignan, when he refused to pay the bribes the representatives demanded. As the story goes, Vesalius was so offended by the event that he spent several weeks, at great expense, petitioning the court for some form of recompense for the disrespect shown to him. Perhaps fueled by the tension of their long and aggravated delay or by the mysterious circumstances of their journey, Andreas and Anne were decidedly at odds by the time they reached Cette (Sete), sixty miles up the French coast. Was the trip proving too dangerous for them to include their daughter? Had Vesalius changed his plans? Was he planning to leave Spain forever? Was it always the plan for the trio to separate early in the trip? Naturally, there are no answers here. What is known is that Vesalius and his family separated at Cette, with his wife and daughter heading on to Brussels, leaving him to continue up the coast to Marseilles, where he planned to take a ship to Genoa and then travel over land to Venice.

It has been suggested that, before Vesalius left Venice for Jerusalem, the Venetian authorities offered Vesalius the chair of anatomy at Padua, as it had remained empty following the death of Fallopio a short time earlier. Although there is no record of this offer, Vesalius had maintained long-standing relations with many of Padua's faculty over the years, and since the *Fabrica* constituted the foundation of the school's anatomical program, it is reasonable to think that Vesalius might have been invited to once again hold the chair that had been named in his honor. In light of the suffocating intellectual atmosphere of Spain, the possibility of returning to the university must have appeared to Vesalius as an opportunity that would allow him to fully pursue his life's ambition: to develop a bridge between anatomical study and clinical medical practice.

v. *The Final Voyage*

There is nothing to suggest that Vesalius's journey to the Holy Land was anything but pleasant; however, the same cannot be said for his return trip to Italy. The passage through Jaffa was the most common and well-traveled route between Venice and Jerusalem, and rather than await the larger ships of the Venetian fleet, Vesalius opted to seek voyage on an independent pilgrim ship. Although one German account accuses Vesalius of choosing a small ship because it constituted cheaper travel—adding also that Vesalius did not provide enough food for the voyage in an attempt to save money—this action does not appear consistent with Vesalius's behavior on previous journeys. What does seem likely, however, is that Vesalius wished to return to Venice before the commencement of a new academic year, the implication being that Vesalius had indeed accepted the position at Padua and was returning to assume his teaching responsibilities.

As the ship made its way into the Adriatic Sea, it encountered a violent storm with winds that battered the vessel for more than thirty days. Supplies quickly became scarce; some passengers became sick, while others died. The German account claims that Vesalius was so frightened by these deaths that his mind became disturbed and "fell ill, first through anxiety and then through fear, and asked that if he should die he might not like the others, become food for the fish."[250] Although dramatic, this tale seems improbable for it is, once again, not consistent with the character of a man who spent his entire life surrounded by the bodies of the dead and the ravages of war. The storyteller's credibility is further undermined by his haughty conclusion: "Therefore, consider how the death of that very famous man will serve you and me and will be an example for many."[251] What one should take from this cryptic warning is between the writer and his imagined reader; however, there appears an unspoken and perhaps displaced aggression in his words that resists deciphering.

By most accounts, when the storm finally ceased, the ship was able to reach a harbor at Zante (now known as Zakynthos), a remote island along the Greek coast within what was then Venetian territory. Vesalius, ill from his travels, went ashore never to return to the ship. The cause and circumstances surrounding Vesalius's death remain as unknown today as the plans he hoped to keep upon his arrival back in Venice.

One writer, in mourning over the loss of Vesalius, stated that he was a "very great philosopher and physician, but in matters of anatomy so rare and singular that it can deservedly be said that he was almost the founder."[252] Vesalius's sudden and severe illness after experiencing great duress at sea, the writer said, clearly demonstrated that "great misery and strange accidents hover over the life of man." Had Vesalius been able to judge his own death as he had so many others, he would most certainly have agreed.

For those of us who prefer to hope that those we care about find a benevolent audience in their last moments, one tale of Vesalius's death adds the following: On the shores of Zante, a wandering Venetian goldsmith happened upon the ailing Vesalius and tried to persuade the islanders to give him aid. Having just endured a recent plague, and fearing another, the locals refused. Under the considerate care of the goldsmith, Vesalius quietly died. Taking Vesalius's body, the goldsmith "with his own hands prepared the grave and buried the body so that it might not remain as food and nourishment for wild beasts." And there he was laid to rest.

In the early winter of 1564, a letter arrived in Madrid, Spain, from a physician colleague, Giovanni Filippo, addressed to "the no-less-learned-than-celebrated Andreas Vesalius, justly the Prince of Anatomists."[253] Although Vesalius would never receive the letter or its greeting, the regal title in its address continues to accompany him today: Andreas Vesalius, the Prince of Anatomists.

EPILOGUE

In the life of Andreas Vesalius, two events that offer the most insight into the man that would, in many respects, become immortal. In legends and myths, the protagonist—the hero—is often one who is not originally on a path to greatness, but through error and misfortune, steps into a potential that would otherwise have remained dormant. In the case of Vesalius, it was his return to Louvain due to the war in France that first threw him from a life ordinary and revealed to him opportunities that would never have arisen had he remained in a more restrictive environment.

At Louvain, Vesalius was not only given the opportunity to develop his dissection skills, but he was also given the freedom and authority to work without the noise of Galenic indoctrination. The result was that for the first time in his life, Vesalius was beginning to *see*. Although he would come to challenge many assumptions derived from orthodox theories, it was in fact his devotion to Galen and Galen's insistence that one should adopt dissection as a means of separating fact from speculation that gave Vesalius the confidence to move unceasingly forward in his work, despite frequent attacks from those who were threatened by his "madness."

The second significant event in Vesalius's life was one far more shattering than the first. Completing his masterwork, the *Fabrica*, which culminated his efforts in medical theory, artistic representation, and exhaustive research, set Vesalius firmly before the emperor's court as a necessary candidate for imperial service. At the very pinnacle of his professional and personal achievements, Vesalius was ready to assume the position that was his familial inheritance. But just as he was about to fulfill this destiny, he tried to flee from it. Fearing that he had made a great error, Vesalius appealed to the emperor for his release, but his request was denied. Devastated at the carelessness with which he had sacrificed his true love, academic study, Vesalius sank into a state of madness, destroying all evidence of his past life. Although many believe Vesalius's public excuse for the event (that it was a response to the extreme criticism he received over the release of the *Fabrica*), as any student of psychology can tell you, the reason someone gives to explain what he has done is never truly the reason.

In the preface to the *Fabrica*, Vesalius states that his desire is to unite medical theory with empirical anatomical research. It is here that Vesalius sows the seeds of the tragic hero. In the old story "Appointment in Samarra," a servant is threatened by Death as he is performing errands for his master in a Baghdad market. Frightened by what he has seen, the servant runs home and tells his master of the scene in the market and begs him for use of a horse so that he may flee to Samarra where Death will not find him. The master allows it and sends his servant away with haste. Angered by what has happened, the master finds Death in the marketplace and asks her why she has threatened his servant. Death responds, "I did not mean to frighten your servant. I only expressed my surprise at seeing him here, when I am to meet him in Samarra tonight." Just as the servant's fate takes into account his attempt to escape his own destiny, Vesalius, though he believed that he was moving away from his destiny, found himself forced to return to imperial service. In the years that followed, while in service to Charles V, Vesalius was not taken from his desire to develop a united medical discipline, but rather was delivered *to* it, through his training on the battlefield and his experience in the emperor's court. But as is the fate of the tragic hero, no sooner was his wish granted to him, than it was taken away.

Should Vesalius have been allowed to assume his chair at the University of Padua in 1564, a medical revolution would most certainly have ensued that would have seen anatomical theory and therapeutic practice joined in a new discipline; however, in the unfortunate absence of Andreas Vesalius, this did not come into being until nearly two centuries after his death. For one such as myself, who meditates regularly on the life of Vesalius and his magnum opus, *De humani corporis fabrica*, I cannot help but wonder what magnificent effort Vesalius would have brought into being, had he been able to put into words and images what he had so successfully manifested in his final practice.

ENDNOTES

1   This quote is from Plate 22 of Andreas Vesalius's *Fabrica* and appears in Latin, engraved upon a tomb.

2   There are numerous versions of this story, but the "madman" that I am thinking of here is from Friedrich Nietzsche's *Thus Spake Zarathustra* in particular.

3   Nietzsche, Friedrich. (1883-85) *Thus Spake Zarathustra*, Prologue 5.

4   In the tradition of humanist scholars and professionals of his time, Vesalius would later adopt the Latin translation of his name, changing Andries van Wesle to Andreas Vesalius Bruxellensis. To avoid confusion, I will refer to Vesalius's father by the Flemish version of his name, Andries van Wesele, and to Andreas Vesalius by his adopted Latin name.

5   A landmark bronze fountain in Brussels, it depicts a small boy peeing into a pool.

6   O'Malley, Charles Donald. (1964). *Andreas Vesalius of Brussels, 1514-1564*. Los Angeles: University of California Press, pp. 21-22.

7   For an interesting account of the role of astrology in sixteenth-century medicine, see Allan Chapman's (1979) "Astrological Medicine," in Charles Webster, (Ed.). *Health, Medicine and Mortality in the Sixteenth Century*. Cambridge University Press.

8   Vesalius's family name appears as Witing (German), Wesele (Flemish), and Vesalius (Latin).

9   This shield of arms was later prominently displayed on the title page of Vesalius's 1543 masterpiece, the *Fabrica*.

10   Copenhaver, Brian P. and Charles B Schmitt. (1992). *Renaissance Philosophy* (New York: Oxford University Press. p. 14.

[11] Eisenstein, Elizabeth. (1980). *The Printing Press as an Agent of Change.* Cambridge University Press.

[12] From Albinia De la Mare, unpublished thesis, "Vesapsiano da Bisticci Historian and Bookseller" quoted in Eisenstein, p. 46. For a discussion of the book as commodity, see Lucien Febvre and Henri-Jean Martin, *The Coming of the Book: The Impact of Printing 1450-1800.* p. 109 ff.

[13] Ibid. pp. 52-53.

[14] Ibid. pp. 107-113.

[15] Ibid. p. 191.

[16] O'Malley (1964). op. cit., pp. 29-31.

[17] Houston, R.A. (1988) *Literacy in Early Modern Europe: Culture and Education*, 1500-1800. Essex: Longman. p. 81.

[18] Ibid. p. 56.

[19] Huntsman, Jeffrey F. (1983) "Grammar," in *The Seven Liberal Arts in the Middle Ages*, David L. Wagner (Ed.) Bloomington: Indiana University Press. p. 58.

[20] Newman, John Henry. (1854) "The Idea of a University," *Modern History Sourcebook*. Retrieved on March 1 from http://www.fordham.edu/halsall/mod/newman/newman-university.html

[21] O'Malley (1964). op. cit., p. 31.

[22] Idem.

[23] Copenhaver, Brian P. and Charles B Schmitt. (1992). *Renaissance Philosophy.* New York: Oxford University Press. p. 1.

[24] Siraisi, Nancy G. (1990). *Medieval and Early Renaissance Medicine: An Introduction to Knowledge and Practice.* University of Chicago Press. pp 65-70 sic passim.

[25] Ibid. p. 67.

[26] Ferguson, Wallace K. (1962). *Europe in Transition, 1300-1520.* Boston: Houghton Mifflin. p. 548.

[27] O'Malley (1964). op. cit., p. 33

[28] Brandi, Karl. (1963). *The Emperor Charles V: The Growth and Destiny of a Man and of a World-Empire.* C. V. Wedgwood (Trans.) London: Jonathan Cape. p. 442.

[29] O'Malley (1964). op. cit., p. 319.

30 Toomer, G. J. (1996). *Eastern Wisdom and Learning: The Study of Arabic in Seventeenth-Century England*. Oxford University Press. p. 41.

31 O'Malley (1964). op. cit., p. 33.

32 Idem.

33 Ibid., p. 37.

34 Ibid. p. 403.

35 Ibid. p. 40

36 This form of direct payment was also necessary for students attending lectures by visiting and guest scholars.

37 Porter, Roy. (1998). *The Greatest Benefit to Mankind: A Medical History of Humanity*. New York: W.W. Norton & Co. Porter. p. 77

38 Singer, Charles Joseph and C. Rabin. (1946). *A Prelude to Modern Science, being a discussion of the history, sources, and circumstances of the "Tabulae anatomicae sex" of Vesalius*. Cambridge University Press (Welcome Historical Medical Museum Publications, New Series No. 1). p. xv.

39 Idem.

40 Vesalius himself would contribute to a later edition (1541) of the *Opera Galeni*, derived from Guinter's translation.

41 Eisenstein. (1980). pp 193-194.

42 Singer and Rabin. (1946). op. cit., pp. xv.

43 Idem.

44 Although Mondino's anatomy text was not included in the University of Paris's curriculum, many Parisian scholars were nonetheless aware of his work. Andres de Laguna, a student colleague of Vesalius's who references Mondino in his own work, speaks to this latent following of the Italian anatomist. Additionally, Vesalius's mentor, Nicholas Florenas, who studied in Bologna, was likely familiar with Mondino's work. If we consider that Mondino was among the first sixteenth-century medical scholars to recommend dissection as the most effective technique for studying anatomy, it is reasonable to surmise that Vesalius was either formally introduced to Mondino through a teacher or associate or was independently drawn to him.

45 Singer and Rabin. (1946). op. cit., p. xv.

46 Nutton, Vivian. (2003) "Historical Introduction," the *Northwestern Translation*. Retrieved on March 1 from http://vesalius.northwestern. edu/books/FA.aa.html.

47 Siraisi (1990). op. cit., p. 77.

48 Nuland, Sherwin B. (1988). *Doctors: The Biography of Medicine*. New York: Vintage Books. p. 72.

49 Galen, *On Anatomcial Procedures*, trans., Charles Singer: London: Oxford Press for Wellcome Historical Medical Museum, 1956, p. 2.

50 Idem.

51 Andreas Vesalius quoted from Garrison, Daniel and Malcom Haste (2003)"Preface," *Northwestern Vesalius*. Retrieved March 1, 2008 from http://vesalius.northwestern.edu/noflash.html, p. 3r.

52 O'Malley (1964). op. cit., p. 55.

53 Ibid., p. 56.

54 Ibid., p. 50-51.

55 Sylvius quoted in Ball, James M. (1910). *Andreas Vesalius, the Reformer of Anatomy*. St. Louis: Medical Science Press. p. 59

56 In Latin: Sylvius hic situs est, gratis qui nil dedit unquam/Mortuus et gratis quod legis ista dolet, quoted in Ball (1910) Idem.

57 O'Malley (1964). op. cit., p. 49.

58 Ibid., p. 53.

59 Ibid., p. 53 and Singer, p 53-57.

60 Sylvius became a member of the faculty in 1556, Vesalius's last year at Paris before returning to Louvain.

61 Garrison and Malcom (2003) "Vesalius on the authority of the authorities," op. cit.

62 Carlino, Andrea. (1999). *Books of the Body: Anatomical Ritual and Renaissance Learning*. John and Anne C. Tedeschi (Trans.). University of Chicago Press.

63 Ibid.

64 Benedetti quoted in Carlino (1999). op. cit., p 219-220.

65 Even today, medical students participate in end-of-term ceremonies that honor the sacrifice of the person whose cadaver they have dissected. It is both a ritual of respect and a cathartic, allowing some student to

STEPHEN N. JOFFE

alleviate himself or herself of guilt for having violated the body/person's dignity through dissection.

66 O'Malley (1964). op. cit., p. 59.

67 Account of Thomas Plater in sixteenth century, Diefendorf, Barbar B. (1991) *Beneath the Cross: Catholics and Huguenots in Sixteenth-Century Paris.* New York: Oxford University Press. p. 13.

68 O'Malley (1964). op. cit., p. 59.

69 Idem.

70 Plater quoted in Loudon, Ervine (Ed.) (1997) *Western Medicine: An Illustrated History.* Oxford University Press. pp. 148-149.

71 O'Malley (1964). op. cit., p. 60.

72 Ibid., p. 58.

73 Ibid., p. 62.

74 D'Aubigne, H.H. Merle. (2005). *History of the Reformation in the Time of Calvin.* Retrieved on March 1, 2008 from http://www.williamtyndale.com. Also see Nicholas Crane's (2003). *Mercator: The Man Who Mapped the Planet.* New York: Henry Holt and Company for more on Tyndale, pp. 77-78.

75 D'Aubigne (2005). op. cit.

76 O'Malley (1964). op. cit., p. 63.

77 Idem.

78 Andreas Vesalius (*Fabrica*) quoted in Saunders, J.B. de C.M. and C. D. O'Malley. (1950) *The Illustrations from the Works of Andreas Vesalius of Brussels.* Cleveland: The World Publishing Company, p. 14.

79 O'Malley (1964). op. cit., p. 64.

80 Idem.

81 Singer and Rabin. (1946). op. cit. p. xxiii.

82 Garrison and Haste (2003). "Preface," op. cit. p. 3r.

83 O'Malley (1964). op. cit., p. 70.

84 Cushing, Harvey W. (1943). *A Bio-Bibliography of Andreas Vesalius.* New York: Yale University. p. 3-4

85 O'Malley (1964). op. cit., p. 70.

86 Idem.

87 Cushing (1943). op. cit., p. 5.

88 Ibid., p. 6.

89 Winter (in partnership with Johannes Oporinus) had also published Guinter's *Institutiones* the previous year.

90 Cushing (1943). op. cit., p. 6.

91 For a full discussion see Paul F. Grendler (2002), *The Universities of the Italian Renaissance*. Baltimore: John Hopkins University Press. pp. 21-40.

92 Grendler (2002). op. cit. p. 23.

93 Norwich John Julius. (1989) *A History of Venice*. New York: Vintage Books. p. 275.

94 Grendler (2002). op. cit., p. 33.

95 Ibid.

96 O'Malley (1964). op. cit., p. 77.

97 O'Malley (1964). op. cit., p. 82.

98 Ibid., p. 81.

99 O'Malley (1964). op. cit., pp 82-83.

100 Alberti, Leon Battista. On Painting. [First appeared 1435-36] Translated with Introduction and Notes by John R. Spencer. New Haven: Yale University Press. 1970 [First printed 1956]. Retrieved on March 1, 2008 from http://www.noteaccess.com/Texts/Alberti/

101 Kemp, Martin. (1997) "Medicine in View: Art and Representation," in *Western Medicine. An Illustrated History*, (ed. I). Loudon, Oxford. p. 3.

102 Carlino (1999). op. cit., p. 199.

103 Idem.

104 Idem.

105 O'Malley (1964). op. cit., p. 19.

106 Vesalius (Tabulae) in Rabin and Singer (1946), op. cit., p.iv.

107 Ibid., p. x

108 Kemp, Martin. (1997) "Medicine in View: Art and Representation," in *Western Medicine. An Illustrated History*, (ed. I). Loudon, Oxford. p. 1.

109 Idem.

110 Idem.

111 Ibid., p. 2.

112 Cushing (1943). op. cit., p. 16.

113 Idem.

114 Idem.

115 Idem.

116 Ibid., p. 21.

117 Singer and Rabin. (1946). op. cit., iii.

118 See Singer and Rabin. (1946). op. cit., pp. xlii-lxiv for extensive discussion on medical misinterpretations.

119 Kemp (1997). op. cit., p. 1-24.

120 Vesalius (*Institutiones*) in Cushing (1943), op. cit., p.45-46.

121 Ibid., p.46.

122 Idem.

123 See Putnam, Haven. (1962). *Books and Their Makers during the Middle Ages: A Study of the Conditions of the Production and Distribution of Literature from the Fall of the Roman Empire to the Close of the Seventeenth Century. Volume: 2.* New York, Hillary House Publishers, for a broader discussion on publishing during the early stages of printing.

124 Febvre and Martin (1997). op. cit., p. 159.

125 Cushing (1943). op. cit., p. 64.

126 For a complete translation of Vesalius's *Venesection Letter*, see Saunders, J.B. de C.M. and C. D. O'Malley. (1947) *Andreas Vesalius Bruxelensis: The Bloodletting Letter of 1539: An Annotated Translation and Study of the Evolution of Vesalius' Scientific Development.* New York: Schuman.

127 Ibid., p. 7.

128 An imprecise term used to describe a variety of conditions thought to derive from inflammation of the lungs and/or the surrounding tissues.

129 An expression of Jeremiah Drivère of Louvain, quoted in Saunders and O'Malley. (1947), pp. 40-41.

130 Saunders and O'Malley (1947). op. cit., p. 44.

131 Ibid., p. 46n110.

132 Ibid., p. 56.

133 Many years later, after further examination, Vesalius concluded that the "fibres had come rather from the imagination of the authors than that they existed in the nature of things." Ibid., p.60n143.

[134] A form of published correspondence.

[135] Saunders and O'Malley (1947). op. cit., p. 40.

[136] Ibid., p. 47

[137] Saunders and O'Malley (1947). op. cit., p. 44.

[138] Ibid., p. 62

[139] Ibid., p. 64.

[140] Ibid., p. 19.

[141] Ibid., p. 40.

[142] Ibid., p. 41.

[143] Ibid. pp. 40-41.

[144] Ibid., p. 88-89.

[145] The appointment of a sympathetic judge, Marcantonio Contarini, allowed more bodies of executed criminals to be made available for dissection.

[146] Saunders and O'Malley (1947). op. cit., p. 7.

[147] Ibid., p. 19.

[148] Ibid., p. 87.

[149] Ibid., p. 34.

[150] Ibid., p. 59 n 143.

[151] O'Malley (1964). op. cit., p. 98.

[152] Eriksson, Ruben. (Ed. and Trans). (1959). *Andreas Vesalius' First Public Anatomy at Bologna, 1540. An Eyewitness Report.* Uppsala and Stockholm: Almqvist & Wiksells, p. 45.

[153] Ibid., p. 137

[154] Ibid., p. 159

[155] The account is an extrapolation from Baldasar Heseler's personal notes, presented in Eriksson (1959). op. cit., pp. 273-275.

[156] The following dialogue is based on Heseler's notes combined with speculative extrapolation.

[157] O'Malley (1964). op. cit., p. 100.

[158] Idem.

[159] Idem.

[160] Idem.

[161] Idem.

[162] Ibid., p. 104.

[163] Idem.

[164] Ibid., p. 105.

[165] Ibid., p. 104.

[166] Ibid., p. 130.

[167] Erikkson (1959). op. cit. p. 139.

[168] O'Malley (1964). op. cit., p. 114.

[169] Idem.

[170] Garrison, Daniel and Malcom Haste (2003) "To the Divine Charles V, the Mightiest and Most Unvanquished Emperor: Andreas Vesalius' PREFACE to his books On the Fabric of the Human Body" the *Northwestern Translation*. Retrieved on March 1 from http://vesalius. northwestern.edu, p. 3r.

[171] O'Malley (1964). op. cit., p. 322.

[172] Cushing (1943). op. cit., p. 81.

[173] Garrison and Haste (2003). "Vesalius on the Authorities of the Authorities," op. cit., p. 1

[174] Ibid., p. 6.

[175] O'Malley (1964). op. cit., p. 322.

[176] Idem.

[177] Garrison and Haste (2003). "Preface," op. cit., p. 5r.

[178] O'Malley (1964). op. cit., p. 124.

[179] For detailed accounts of the business of art during the Renaissance, see Cole, Bruce. (1983). *The Renaissance Artist at Work: From Pisano to Titian*. New York: Harper and Row; and Baxandall, Michael *Painting & Experience in Fifteenth Century Italy: A primer in the social history of pictorial style, 2nd Ed.* Oxford University Press.

[180] For a complete account see King, Ross. (2002). *Michelangelo and the Pope's Ceiling*. London: Chatto and Windus.

[181] O'Malley (1964). op. cit., p. 126.

[182] Garrison and Haste (2003). "Preface," op. cit., p. 6.

[183] E. Jackschath, "Zu den anatominchen Abbildungen des Vesale" quoted in O'Malley (1934). op. cit., p. 439.

[184] Ibid., p. 128

[185] Kemp (1997). op. cit., p. 1-24.

[186] Leppert, Richard D. (1996). *Art and the Committed Eye: The Cultural Functions of Imagery.* Boulder, CO: Westview Press. pg. 123.

[187] Ibid.

[188] Ibid., pp.127-129.

[189] Sawday, Jonathan. (1993). *The Body Emblazoned: Dissection and the Human Body in Renaissance Culture.* p. 115.

[190] Idem.

[191] O'Malley (1964). op. cit., p. 108.

[192] Cushing (1943). op. cit., p. 76.

[193] The following biographical account of Oporinus's life is derived from O'Malley (1964), op. cit., pp. 131-133 and Steingberg, S.H. and John Trevitt. (1996). *Five Hundred Years of Printing.* London: British Library.

[194] Steingberg, S.H. and John Trevitt.(1996). Op. cit., p. 22.

[195] In the sixteenth century, these three territories were identified as the Province of Basel of the Swiss Confederacy, the State of Freiburg of the Roman Catholic Empire, and the Franche Comte, long part of the Burgundian dominion.

[196] Garrison and Haste (2003), "Preface," op. cit., p. 4r.

[197] This account is derived from O'Malley (1964). op. cit., pp. 137-138.

[198] Gauffering produces a fluted or crimped design, usually by the application of a hot iron.

[199] The following account of Charles V is largely derived from Brandi, Karl. (1963). *The Emperor Charles V: The Growth and Destiny of a Man and of a World-Empire.* C. V. Wedgwood (Trans.) London: Jonathan Cape.

[200] Brandi (1963). op. cit., p. 476.

[201] Ibid., p. 477.

[202] Nutton (2003), "The Book," op. cit.

[203] Nutton (2003). op. cit.

[204] Idem.

[205] Idem.

[206] Idem.

207 Garrison and Haste (2003), "Preface," op. cit., p. 3r.

208 Idem.

209 Nutton (2003). op. cit.

210 Vesalius quoted in Cushing(1943). op. cit., p. 162.

211 Sylvius (*Vaesanus*) quoted in Cushing (1943). op. cit., p.xxx.

212 Henerus quoted in O'Malley (1964). op. cit., p. 247.

213 This reviewed appeared in a preface that Gamusaeus wrote for a small text on fevers written by Antonio Fumanelli. Nutton (2003). op. cit., p. 22-23.

214 Idem.

215 Idem.

216 Vesalius (*Letter on the China Root*) as translated by O'Malley (1964). op. cit., p. 197.

217 Leonard Fuch's "Introduction to De humani corporis fabric ex Galeni & Andreae Vesalii libris concinnatae epitome," quoted in O'Malley, p. 245.

218 Ibid., pp. 245-246.

219 Nutton (2003). op. cit.

220 O'Malley (1964). op. cit., p. 218.

221 O'Connell, Robert L. (1989). *Of Arms and Men: A History of War, Weapons and Aggression*. New York: Oxford University Press. p. 113.

222 O'Malley (1964). op. cit., p. 197.

223 Ibid., p.198.

224 O'Malley (2003). op. cit., p. 201.

225 Ibid., p. 200

226 Idem.

227 Ibid., p. 196.

228 O'Malley (1964). op. cit., p. 191.

229 Ibid., pp. 194-195.

230 Blockmans (2001), op. cit.

231 O'Malley (1964). op. cit., p. 215.

232 Garrison and Haste (2003). op cit., p. 2r.

233 Chacon quoted in O'Malley (1964). op. cit., p. 209.

234 Brandi (1963). op. cit., p. 591.

235 Ibid. p. 592

236 O'Malley (1964). op. cit., p. 264-265.

237 Ibid., p. 265.

238 Idem.

239 O'Malley (1964). op. cit., pp. 390-91.

240 O'Malley (1964). op. cit., p. 218.

241 Ibid., p. 257.

242 Ibid., p. 396.

243 Pierson, Peter (1975). *Philip II of Spain*. London: Thames & Hudson. p. 61.

244 Idem.

245 Ibid., p. 11.

246 Idem.

247 O'Malley (1964). op. cit., p. 304.

248 Ibid., p. 469.

249 O'Malley (1964). op. cit., p. 306.

250 Ibid.

251 Johann Metellus (1565) quoted in O'Malley (1964). op. cit., p. 311.

252 Pietro Bizzari (1568) quoted in O'Malley (1964). Op. cit., p. 309.

253 Ibid., p. 419.

Printed in Great Britain
by Amazon

48657727R00125